Chico Xavier
Stories of a friend from another land

An imprint of RMF books
6136 NW 53rd Circle, Coral Springs, FL 33067, USA.
E-mail: contact@rmfbooks.com - rmf@rmfbooks.com

Copyright © 2013 Umberto Fabbri

All rights reserved. Except for brief quotations in critical articles or reviews, no part of this book may be reproduced in any manner without prior written permission from the author.

1st Edition by RMFbooks, 2014

The rights of Umberto Fabbri as author have been asserted in accordance with the Copyright, Designs and Patents Act 1988.

International Cataloguing Information in Publication
Fabbri, Umberto
Chico Xavier - Stories of a friend from another land
Umberto Fabbri - Florida - US

For information about bulk discounts or to purchase copies of this book, please contact RMFbooks at 954-345-9790 or contact@rmfbooks.com

Translation by John Jensen with revision by Jennifer L. Jensen from original Portuguese-language edition © 2013 John Jensen
Manufactured in the United States of America

10 9 8 7 6 5 4 3 2 [1]

348p;

ISBN 978-0692231616 Paperback

CHICO ♥ XAVIER

Stories of a friend from another land

Table of Contents

Chapter 1
First Encounter 17
The Prayer Spiritist Group 21
Charity 25

Chapter 2
Augusto Cezar Neto Home Workshop 29

Chapter 3
February 1983 33
Out of body 36
Thought 37

Chapter 4
The Avocado Tree 43
Beneficence 44
Detachment 45

Chapter 5
Reading of Thoughts 47
Scientists develop a technique to "read" thoughts ... 50
Images and Sounds 51
Secret Word 51

Chapter 6
Reading Thoughts and Mental Responses 53

  Telepathy 56

Chapter 7
  Fluidified Water in the Gospel at Home 59
  Water 61
  Fluidified Water 62
  Ectoplasm 63

Chapter 8
  Unexpected Visit 69
  Ectoplasm 70
  Perispirit 71

Chapter 9
  The Snake Around the Neck 75
  Vibration 79
  Ovoid 79

Chapter 10
  A Spirit in Need 83
  Spirits that are unaware of their own situation ... 85
  Suffering Spirits 85

Chapter 11
  Gospel in the Pocket 87
  Evil speaking 89
  Evil Speaker 89

Chapter 12
  Trial or Atonement? 91
  Suicide 93

  Helpful pain 95
Chapter 13
  Food for the Cats 97
  Patience 98
Chapter 14
  The Line 103
  Mediunic Mandate 106
Chapter 15
  Dom Pedro II's Chef 125
  Friendship 126
Chapter 16
  The Cat and the Bird 127
  To work 129
Chapter 17
  The Banana 131
  Astral Body 132
  Disincarnation 133
Chapter 18
  Two Hundred Years of Violence? 135
  Violence 136
Chapter 19
  The Cart 139
  Disincarnation 140
Chapter 20
  The Machine 143

    Patience 146
    Calm 146
    Vigilance 146
    Tolerance 147

Chapter 21
    Little Message Boxes 149
    Psychometrist 151
    Psychometry 152

Chapter 22
    Spiritist Center in the Lower Zone 157
    Lower Zone 158

Chapter 23
    Full of Cats 161
    Spiritist book 163

Chapter 24
    Different Stories with the Same Ending 165
    Trial 171
    Atonement 172

Chapter 25
    ET's or Interpretations? 175
    Mystification 177
    Mystifier 178

Chapter 26
    Son of Emmanuel 179
    Emmanuel 180

Dr. Bezerra de Menezes 182

Chapter 27
The Moon 185
The Guilty 187
Evil 187

Chapter 28
Message for Mothers 189
Relationships 191

Chapter 29
Organ Donation 195
Organ Donation and Transplants 197
Organ Transplant and Codification 198
Psychosomatic Rejection 201
Organ Donation: Material Disconnection 202
Conclusion 204

Chapter 30
The Heart in the Wallet 207
Mechanical Mediumship 209

Chapter 31
The Room-Message for a Mother 211
Psychography [also known as automatic writing] .213
Resignation 215

Chapter 32
The Inebriated Driver 217
Free Agency 221

VICE	222
ALCOHOL	222
ALCOHOLIC	223
ALCOHOLICS AND DRUG ADDICTS	224
OBSESSION	224

Chapter 33

PAUL AND STEVEN	225
SEER AND HEARER MEDIUMS	227
SEERS	227
HEARERS	228

Chapter 34

THE UBERABA PENITENTIARY	231
OBSESSION	234

Chapter 35

ACCOMPANYING CHICO	239
PERFUME	242

Chapter 36

QUESTIONS ABOUT HITLER AND ANDRÉ LUIZ	245
DR. CARLOS CHAGAS	247

Chapter 37

SEVEN OBSESSORS FOR EACH	271
OBSESSION	275
FORGIVENESS	280

Chapter 38

ONE OF THE STORIES ABOUT BRINQUINHO THE DOG	283

    The animals of Jupiter 287
    Gospel at Home 288

Chapter 39
    Chico's Visits in Dreams 299
    Leaving the Body and Bilocation 299
    Spiritist Dreams 300

Chapter 40
    The Desk at the Prayer Spiritist Group 305

Chapter 41
    The Cockroach 309
    Concentration 310
    Discipline 311

Chapter 42
    The Verses of Jair Presente 313
    Lack of Vigilance 315
    Service 316
    Spiritist Social Service 316
    To Serve 317

Chapter 43
    Visit to the Cemetery 319
    Perturbation in Disincarnation 322

Chapter 44
    Antusa and Her Blessings 323
    Blessing by the laying on of hands 325

Chapter 45
Mrs. Aparecida and the Pênfigo Hospital 331
Stationary Debt 333

Chapter 46
A Mother's Heart 343
Heart 344
Mother's Heart 345

How This Book Came About

Dear Reader,

It is with great joy that I present this unique work. Without literary pretensions, my intention is to share one of the greatest treasures of my life: my twenty-year close relationship with Francisco Cândido Xavier, our beloved Chico, who was an example of love, intelligence, and goodness.

I had never considered writing a book before. My activities in the Spiritist movement have always centered on the Doctrine, disseminating and teaching it through speeches or lectures for regular Spiritism courses.

Professionally, I have always been in marketing or sales, which requires no great literary talent; and thus,

I am a novice scribe on his first sojourn.

A while ago, a friend of mine, Mário Celso Antunes, who is a fellow proselytizer of Spiritism, a frequent participant in the Prayer Spiritist Group, and a visitor to Chico's home, encouraged me to write this book so I could pass on the marvelous lessons I learned from this great man and missionary, Cândido.

My time with the great missionary was spent in great simplicity. But, as Antunes rhetorically asked: Why should great lessons happen only on special occasions? Remember the world's most remarkable examples of love, for which all the great missionaries, without exception, had simple teachings full of clear objective examples.

At first, I refused my friend's suggestion because of my lack of writing experience, and because Chico had already been the subject of many biographies by very competent writers.

He responded with the further suggestion that I seek out cases which had not been written about yet, or if they had been, to add new insights or forgotten episodes from the past .

Simplicity was part of Chico's nature, despite his grandiose mission which I discovered during one of my first visits to him. At one point, he referred to himself by saying:

"Look at my name: Francisco

If you take off Fran, only Cisco [speck] remains."

I decided to use that exact phrase as the title of this unpretentious book. I dedicate this work to that great soul, an example of the purest of love, and to whom I owe much of what I am.

I hope it may be as inspirational for you as it has been for me.

Chapter 1

First Encounter

When I was 26 years old, on a sunny Wednesday morning, December 15, 1982, I arrived in Uberaba, Minas Gerais state, after traveling for most of the night. The trip was hard and long because the Anhanguera highway, connecting São Paulo and Minas Gerais, had one lane and was full of cars and trucks.

What an adventure we had! My friends, Mário and Samuel, and I drove the almost 300 miles in Mario's Ford Corcel, which had seen better days. We called his car the "Batmobile" because it was fast? No, because it was really old!

The month of December was very special for the Prayer Spiritist Group while under the direction of Chico Xavier. It was the month of the great Christmas distribution. So, we were part of the Augusto Cezar Home Workshop, led by our beloved Mrs. Yolanda Cezar, who was in charge of distribution: trousseaus, baskets of food, toys, fruit, and bread, as well as some money which Chico distributed himself. We were in Uberaba for this reason, to contribute, to be useful, and to have the "honor of serving," as we were taught by Emmanuel, Chico Xavier's mentor.

On that Wednesday evening, we were planning to visit Chico at his home. The small caravan left the hotel in the direction of his house, with Mrs. Yolanda's car at the front leading the way. We entered the house and went into a room at the back which had a long table and wooden benches. Everything was very simple, just like the rest of the house.

Suddenly, that brilliant figure appeared, accompanied by Mrs. Yolanda, with his great magnetism spawned from his capacity for love, which evolved spirits have. Because of our own smallness and limitations, we could not truly appraise the great man, who was small in stature but a spiritual giant.

My emotions were a mixture of admiration, responsibility, and shyness. We were facing the medium who had psychographed the first Spiritist book I ever read, Nosso Lar[1] by André Luiz, which led me to the Spiritist Doctrine. Also facing me was one of the greatest examples of compassion for one's neighbor, living as Jesus taught us.

Why not Cisco?

Years later, while conversing with a friend, Gláucio, who was part of the Augusto Cezar Home Workshop, I made the comment, "Look, we've been to Chico's house several times, where we played around and were happy to be among friends and companions, where we were certainly being watched by Emmanuel."

And my friend added: "By Emmanuel, maybe by Jesus himself."

Gláucio was not referring to us, but to Chico, who, because of his great calling and elevation, enjoyed the protection of the highest spiritual spheres; however, we are not encouraging any notion of deification or mysticism of the medium.

Why not by Jesus? Chico, with his irrepressible mediunic quality, was the intermediary in the writing of an extensive collection of more than four hundred books, which greatly contributed to the Doctrine of the Spirits. He intermediated in the communication

---

1 *Nosso Lar* means "Our Home" but the Portuguese title has been retained in translations of the book as well as in its film version, and will be used here.

of such valorous spirits as: Humberto de Campos, Auta de Souza, Maria Dolores, Sheila, Meimei, Anália Franco, and Bezerra de Menezes. Additionally, a great part of those published works were brought forth by Emmanuel who worked on the philosophical and theological segments, and by André Luiz, who worked on the scientific segments.

It was our first direct contact with Chico, and we were anxious, waiting for an opportunity to see him psychographing[2]. The medium did, for hours, from 8:00 p.m. to 2:30 a.m. How many messages of comfort for some of the mothers who were present! And how much learning for us!

Once the meeting was over, which would be repeated the next day, in the same style and with similar hours, Mrs. Yolanda told us that it was time to return to the hotel, and Chico responded:

"Yolanda, leave the boys here a little longer so we can talk."

"A little longer" turned into blessed hours, when he honored us with his knowledge and friendship. There were three or four of us, all thirsty to receive knowledge from such an enlightened being. As Chico

---

2 *Psychographing,* also known as *automatic writing* in English, is the process of transcribing materials dictated by spirits.

spoke to us about Spiritism, politics, and sociology, among other things, we asked ourselves:

"What spirit is this? Who had barely studied anything in this incarnation, only completing the fourth grade which he had to repeat, and yet, who has such deep knowledge? A real wise man!"

We were not facing the medium Chico Xavier, but the man Chico, who demonstrated his deep knowledge of matters of the greatest relevance for the world, holding firm and balanced positions.

There are those who say that our Chico was not just a medium. My God! Mediumship was part of his life, but he could not be only a medium. Before us we had a missionary, who had such great humility that he made jokes about himself, and who also tried to reduce his own brilliance to make the Doctrine even brighter.

Remember his famous phrase: "See my name, I'm called Francisco; taking away the Fran, what is left is just Cisco." ['speck' in Portuguese]

Ah, Chico! I wonder: if you are a cisco, my God, what am I?

The Prayer Spiritist Group

We were present for Friday's work in the Prayer Spiritist Group, where an enormous number of people would seek out the medium, and through his automatic writing, the Spirit Dr. Bezerra de Menezes, would give his homeopathic prescriptions for the health problems of thousands of people who came to the Center.

It was out first visit and we watched everything with great wonder.

Finally, the Christmas distribution!

The trucks arrived at the end of Friday afternoon. Yes, there were trucks that the Augusto Cezar Home Workshop had sent to Uberaba, packed by hundreds of people, who understood the need to practice charity. The trucks were packed with food baskets and toys, but we bought perishable products like fruit, bread and milk, in Uberaba. We would serve a line of 15,000 people, which in a few years would become a line of 25,000 or 30,000 needy people.

The Prayer Spiritist Group's preparation was done after the Friday night session. We unloaded the trucks at dawn so we could begin distribution on Saturday morning, around 6:00 a.m.

We had just one night of preparation to receive people, in lines that would go on for a week! We received mothers and children in misery, women with babes in arms, people in need of almost everything, and hungry teenagers. All of them were waiting, not just for the distribution, but also to kiss the hands of "Uncle Chico," who reciprocated, kissing the hands of these needy people.

I don't remember who, but one person came to visit Chico, and when he saw that his lips were bloody from kissing the hands of so many people, asked him: "Chico, why do you kiss the hands of all the people who come here to visit you?"

Chico answered: "Because I don't have the strength to bend down and kiss their feet."

In the gigantic line, where so much pain was seen in the people's tired eyes, we found a reflection of the lack of love for our brothers. Unfortunately, we still fail to follow the teachings of Jesus: "Love one another as I have loved you." (John 15:12).

The distribution began early in the morning, after prayer with Chico. Curiously, when the medium arrived, the people's tiredness would seem to disappear like magic. It was his energy, the vibration of his aura that encircled us. NASA scientists had already proven that the aura of Chico varied from fifty to sixty feet from his body, while in most people it is no greater than eight inches.

We expected to end the distribution at noon or

1:00 pm. It was intolerably hot, many people were exhausted, waiting for our precious help. Sometimes there were opportunists trying to create confusion in order to get ahead of those people who had suffered rain and sun for days. So everything would stop. Then they would try to reestablish order, police officers helping set up ropes to hold back the crowd. A fire truck sprayed water nicely over all of us to cool us down, and to prevent people from fainting. But there were inevitably some cases of fainting.

Once the line was reestablished, the distribution started again. Chico remained serene and transmitted a feeling of calmness to everyone. The re-organization was done, and it was as if the crowd had received a collective blessing so everyone remained at peace. It was quite impressive. At the end of the afternoon, we were all exhausted. Feeling overwhelmed at the immensity of the work, I said to a colleague:

"I can't come back to Uberaba any more. It's crazy here!"

Then we remembered the wise words of Emmanuel: "We are constant in our inconstancy!" It's good that we did, because in February, exactly two months later, we went back to Uberaba, and continued to visit for more than twenty years, at intervals of 45 to 60 days.

BIBLIOGRAPHICAL REFERENCES FOR RESEARCH

Charity

[…] the word has a very wide meaning. There is charity in thought, and in words, in actions; it does not consist only of giving alms. Someone is charitable in thought, being indulgent with his neighbor's faults; charitable in words, saying nothing that could harm another; charitable in actions when he helps his neighbor as much as he can. The poor man who shares his crumb of bread with someone who is even poorer is more charitable and has more merit in the eyes of God than he who gives superfluously, without depriving himself of anything.

[…] Charity is the opposite of selfishness; the former is the abnegation of one's personality, the latter is exaltation of the personality. One says: "For you first, then for me;" and the other says "For me first, for you whatever is left over." The first is complete in the words of Christ: Do unto others as you would have them do unto you." In a word, it applies without exception to all social relationships […]

Allan Kardec. *Viagem Espírita em 1862 e Outras Viagens de Kardec* **(speeches). Rio de Janeiro, FEB,**

2005. [*Spiritist Trip in 1862 and Other Trips by Kardec*]³

Charity [...] constitutes the moment of maximum wisdom, when the being, freeing itself from the ties that keep it at the rear, as a result of a long evolutionary journey, aspiring to reach the mount of spiritual sublimation, free from any impediment, and light like the peace that is to transform it.

Charity reveals the interior Christ, because it becomes the essence of reality, superior to organic phenomena, lying in the subtle areas of the sublime vibrations of Spirituality.

Divaldo P. Franco. *Impermanência e Imortalidade.* **By the Spirit Carlos Torres Pastorino. 4th ed. Rio de Janeiro: FEB, 2005.** [*Impermance and Immortality*]

Charity is a sublime blessing that unfolds in silent help.

Divaldo P. Franco. *Lampadário Espírita.* **By the**

---

3 Book titles are given as in the original Brazilian edition, but have been translated literally into English in brackets after the reference, but not necessarily the exact title that may be used in a translated edition. This is done in order for the reader to have a sense of the work and to make it possible to find it, should an English-language version be available. Where possible, published English translations of standard Spiritist works have been quoted; in such cases, the title and publication information refer to the translation consulted. Where there is no such reference to an English translation, the text has been rendered from the Portuguese, even when originally written in a third language, such as French or Italian.

Spirit Joanna de Ângelis. 7th ed. Rio de Janeiro: FEB, 2005 [*Spiritist Lamppost*]

… charity, legitimate and pure, is love always alive, flowing incessantly from the love of God.

Francisco Cândido Xavier. *Religião dos Espíritos.* **By the Spirit Emmanuel (Dizes-te) 18th ed. Rio de Janeiro: FEB, 2006. [*Religion of the Spirits*]**

Chapter 2

Augusto Cezar Neto Home Workshop

Our first contact with the Home Workshop occurred during our first visit to Uberaba, as described in the previous chapter.

The Home Workshop was founded on June 7, 1982 by Raul Cezar and Yolanda Cezar, whose children are Marli Cezar Bourgogne, Zuleika Cezar de Carvalho, Maria Otilia Cezar Toscano and Augusto Cesar Neto, who is now on the spiritual plane.

Raul has since returned to the spiritual plane and Mrs. Yolanda, an exemplary worker for Jesus, continues to head the Home Workshop today, with her many 'Januaries of age', to paraphrase our beloved Chico.

The Home Workshop is a charitable Spiritist institution and it was named for Augusto Cezar Neto, who disincarnated in the city of Santos on February 26, 1968 at the age of twenty-six.

The activities of the Home Workshop involve: spiritual assistance, meeting a great variety of social needs, and resources of the Prayer Spiritist Group like food, clothing, trousseaus, etc... The Prayer Spiritist Group is an institution founded and directed by our dear Chico Xavier.

It is worth remembering that Augusto Cezar (Spirit) with great wisdom involved many others in the great work: his parents, his sisters, nieces and nephews, Mrs. Yolanda's grandchildren, sons-in-law, friends, and volunteers who joined the group, who all continue working with inspiration in the noble cause of the Gospel of Jesus.

The truth is that in addition to becoming part of the Spiritist Group, we also joined the beautiful and loving Augusto Cezar family.

Augusto Cezar Neto

Chapter 3

February 1983

Exactly two months later we were on our way once again to Uberaba. The meetings at Chico's home were the same as always: fantastic and educational.

On a Thursday evening at this house, we had a special moment when Chico told us about his experience in his visit to Nosso Lar, 'Our Home.' [Spiritist designation for one part of Heaven]

Chico told us that the new ideas shown by the Spirit André Luiz were so great that his mentor Emmanuel invited the medium to a visit to Nosso Lar, while he was sleeping. Emmanuel asked that the medium observe a special diet for a week so that his separation from his body would be more tranquil. He was to eat as little as possible. After the period of preparation, Emmanuel reported that the trip was ready.

Chico then said:

"Around midnight I fell asleep. I remember that Emmanuel led me to a type of space ship, which at that time, in the 1940's, looked like a Concorde airplane."

Remember that the jet plane appeared only during the Second World War (1939-1945), although designs had existed since the 1930's. The supersonic Concorde airplane, of French origin, would only appear many decades after jet planes were first built.

He said: "When the ship arrived, there were already passengers on board, mostly incarnate souls who were out of body during their sleep."

The ship left very quickly and the most impressive thing is that at a certain moment, Chico realized that the vehicle also was able to move (notice this, reader!) under water and it left in the direction of Nosso Lar, under the sea.

If we had heard a story like this from someone else, we would say it was science fiction. But, because of the information from Chico and advances made in research on other dimensions, we are more and more impressed with the possibilities and surprises within our Universe.

Then Chico confirmed the words in André Luiz's book telling of the beauties of the landscapes, houses, and nocturnal illumination, some of which came from plants and flowers radiating light. But the best was yet to come. Mrs. Yolanda, the leader of our group, asked about the food in the city, which Chico answered in the same way as the Spirit did in Luiz's book.

While Chico spoke of food, I thought: "If they eat in Nosso Lar, could the digestive process be the same as ours?" Notice: we said, "I thought."

Chico excused himself briefly from Mrs. Yolanda and turned to me: "Depending on the evolution of the spirit, the excess is eliminated through the pores, or in most cases, it happens as with us." He had read my thoughts. After that I have often thought to myself: Had he read all of my thoughts? Certainly he had, but, due to his love and respect for others, he would never do anything untoward.

I had believed the lesson was complete for the night, but it had not ended yet. After some minutes of excited conversation, he said to Mrs. Yolanda:

"Do you know, Yolanda, that it now seems like I am hearing his voice with that way of starting a sentence like people from Minas Gerais - sometimes when I am psychographing I leave my body and get close to people and see what they are thinking so that I can help them."

That was the end. I gave up worrying about it and I thought to myself, because I was very young, not yet 27:

"How little control I had of my shameful thoughts?" OR "Oh, how shameful; I should have controlled my thoughts better."

BIBLIOGRAPHICAL REFERENCES FOR RESEARCH

Out of body

[...] it is at the same time fluidic, sensorial and psychic (bilocation), dislocating the conscious personality from the sensitive to the fluidic body, which then perceives, at a distance, his own physical body, inanimate and lifeless [...}

Ernesto Bozzano. *Fenômenos Psíquicos no Momento da Morte*. Trans. by Carlos Imbassahy. 6th ed. Rio de Janeiro: FEB, 2005. Chapter 14. [*Psychic Phenomena at the Time of Death*]

The fundamental law of going out of body is thus enunciated by Mr. Muldoon: "When the subconscious becomes possessed by the idea of movement of the physical body which is unable to do so, the astral body leaves the physical." […]

Miranda, Hermínio C. . *Sobrevivência e Comunicabilidade dos Espíritos.* **4ᵗʰ ed. Rio de Janeiro: FEB, 2002. Chapter 3. [***Survival and Communicability of Spirits***]**

[…] The mechanism of going out of body (during sleep) is simple: the perispirit raises itself horizontally over the physical body, it floats gently in the direction of the head to the feet and it gradually stands on its feet. A sliver thread continues connecting the perispirit to the physical body, whatever distance is covered away from it. […]

***Ibid.*, Chapter 8.**

Going out of body is a natural action of the incarnate spirit which, during repose of the physical body, partially recovers its freedom. **Schubert, Suely Caldas.** *Testemunhos de Chico Xavier. Um Sonho que se Realizou.* **3ʳᵈ ed. Rio de Janeiro: FEB, 1998. [***Testimonies of Chico Xavier. A Dream that Came True***]**

Thought

In normal thought the excitation of the "entire mental atoms" will produce very long waves.

In a state of attention or peaceful tension, caused by "mental electrons," by virtue of reflection or natural prayer, the field of thought will be expressed in medium-length waves.

In extraordinary mental situations, excitation of the tiny "mental atomic nuclei," whatever they are, when in deep emotions, indivisible pains, or laborious and suffering concentrations of mental force of afflictive supplications, the dominion of thought will emit very short waves, theoretically similar to those that approach gamma rays.

Xavier, Francisco Cândido. *Mecanismos da Mediunidade*. By the Spirit André Luiz. 24th ed. Rio de Janeiro: FEB, 2004. [*Mechanisms of Mediumship*]

Thought is, without doubt, the creative force of our own soul and, for this reason, it is the continuation of us. Through it, we function in the environment in which we live and act, setting the pattern of our influence, for good or for evil.

Xavier, Francisco Cândido. *Libertação*. By the Spirit André Luiz. 29th ed. Rio de Janeiro: FEB, 2005. [*Liberation*]

Thought is the creative force, to be revealed to the exterior of the creature that generates it, through subtle waves, in circuits of action and reaction in time, being as measurable as the photon that throws through the luminescent fulcrum that produces it, goes through space at a determined speed, sustaining the sparkling outcome of Creation.

Xavier, Francisco Cândido. *Pensamento e Vida*. By the Spirit Emmanuel. 16th ed. Rio de Janeiro: FEB, 2006. [*Thought and Life*]

Thought is the generator of the infra corpuscles or of the lines of force of the subatomic world, creator of currents of good or of evil, greatness or decadence, life or death, according to the will that exteriorizes it or directs it. [...]

Xavier, Francisco Cândido. *Roteiro*. By the Spirit Emmanuel. 11th ed. Rio de Janeiro: FEB, 2004. Chapter 30. *[Route]*

According to Aristotle, formal thought was governed by four fundamental laws: a) Law of association by simultaneity or temporal continuity; b) Law of association by spatial contiguity; c) Law of association by similarity or contrast of form; d) Law of association by similarities or contrasts of meaning. Nonetheless, these laws do not explain the heart of the matter, that is, the act of thinking, or of the contents of this act or effect obtained therefrom.

According to Mira Y. Lopez, thought remains intimately connected to feelings and to action. Thus, thought does not appear suddenly in phylogenetic evolution, but rather it evolved with the nervous centers that serve it as a substratum. This biological evolution of thought, in particular, and of the spirit, in general, occurred in parallel in the physical and spiritual binomial matter, according to the Spiritist Doctrine, as told by André Luiz [Evolution in Two Worlds].

According to this author, this parallelism occurs between "the spiritual body ... which is not a reflection of the physical body, because, in reality, it is the physical body that reflects the spiritual, just as it, the spiritual body, portrays in itself the mental body that presides over its formation."

Balduino, Leopoldo. *Psiquiatria e Mediunismo.* **2nd ed. Rio de Janeiro: FEB, 1995. Chapter 3.** *[Psychiatry and Mediumship]*

Chico Xavier and Ms. Yolanda Cezar

Chapter 4

The Avocado Tree

In the month of February, we had the opportunity to meet the avocado tree, in the Vila dos Pássaros, also in Uberaba. At the time, under a simple tiled roof, Chico was doing the Gospel with us and then we began the food distribution, with the medium himself donating some money to the neediest people.

Chico's profound respect toward everyone distinguished his trajectory of light. It was a lesson of true sharing and goodness, because the charity collections (gifts and money) from our group were handed over by him in the same way that he received them, without his even opening the envelopes or the gifts. In an interview, the medium declared that the envelopes given to him with donations were never opened by him. All of them, without exception, were passed on intact, just as they had been received. He was a true example of detachment, beginning with small things and then culminating in his donation of all his book royalties. The medium could have been a millionaire, if not for these donations.

BIBLIOGRAPHICAL REFERENCES FOR RESEARCH

Beneficence

Beneficence or charity carried out without ostentation has double merit. In addition to consisting of material charity, it is moral charity, since it protects the susceptibility of the beneficiary, it allows him to accept the benefit without resentment toward his own self-esteem and protecting the dignity of the man, since accepting a service is very different from accepting alms. […]

Kardec, Allan. *O Evangelho Segundo o Espiritismo.* **Trans. by J. Herculano Pires. São Paulo: Edições FEESP, 1970.** [*The Gospel According to Spiritism*]

Beneficence is not only the dispensing of a solution to problems of a material order, but it is much more; it is first aid for the poverty of spirit.

Xavier, Francisco Cândido. *Rumo Certo.* **By the Spirit Emmanuel. 7th ed. Rio de Janeiro: FEB,**

2005. [*Correct Pathway*]

Detachment
[...] Detachment from earthly goods consists in appreciating them for their true value, in knowing how to use them in benefit of others, and not to sacrifice the interests of a future life for them, in losing them without murmuring, should God choose to take them away. [...]
Kardec, Allan. *op. cit.*

Disincarnating in no way frees one who has sublimated himself to whim or rebellion, stubbornness or passion. In this detail, detachment is also a means to retake the path.
Franco, Divaldo P. *Lampadário Espírita.* **By the Spirit Joanna de Ângelis. 7th ed. Rio de Janeiro: FEB, 2005.** [*Spiritist Lamppost*]

Food distribution at the avocado tree

Chapter 5

Reading of Thoughts

Regarding the reading of thoughts, I had had a prior experience concerning the food in Nosso Lar, but that was not the only one. A friend of ours, Ademar, on his first visit to Chico's home in the Uberaba summer, was wearing a polo shirt. He had a habit of carrying a guide [a string of spiritually protective beads], used by many friends who attended Umbanda sessions.

He declared later that before entering the medium's home he thought: "I don't know Chico, and I don't know how he is going to react to the fact that I am using a guide." He was worried about what Chico would think of him.

We open a parenthesis here in relation to Chico Xavier's position in regard to other religions, cults, sects, etc. We always observed a posture of great respect for everything and everyone. Chico, in fact, became ecumenical over time, which is typical of great souls who only "love."

And our friend Ademar, who is on the spiritual plane today, not wanting to annoy Chico, took the guide off his neck and put it in his pocket before entering the medium's home.

Ademar and another companion from the Augusto Cezar Group, both already in the living room, were surprised at Chico's sudden arrival. The friend, who had known Chico for some time, introduced Ademar, saying: "Chico, this is our brother Ademar, who is coming with us, and with the other friends from the Augusto Cezar group…"

Looking at Ademar, Chico greeted him and said: "Ademar, our Ademar from the sea…"Chico was making an allusion to the figure of Yemenjá [goddess of the sea], whom Ademar admired a great deal. And he continued: "It is a pleasure to meet you and receive you here in our home. It brings me great happiness… But, Ademar, the guide that you put in your pocket is supposed to be worn around your neck…" Impressively, Chico had read Ademar's thoughts while a yard away from him.

It is necessary to make an observation about Ademar, this valuable worker for Jesus. Ademar worked for some years at the FEESP – The Spiritist Federation of the State of São Paulo - giving blessings and also acting in the Auta de Souza Campaign, which collects food for charity. Ademar had initiated one of the projects in providing large-scale services for needy people and the homeless, taking food, clothing, and basic supplies to makeshift dwellings under bridges, serving as an example of Christian charity benefitting our needy brethren.

A SIMILAR EVENT

On another occasion, the work on Saturday night had ended and Chico had already said good-bye to everyone, more than four or five hundred people. Many of them simply wouldn't leave. Chico was leaving the Prayer Spiritist Group, always surrounded by an enormous number of people. Some wanted a few more words, others advice, and still others wanted to kiss the medium one more time. Their prolonged farewells were treated with great affection and respect by Chico.

On that night a remarkable event occurred. A journalist who was at the meeting from its beginning was standing up near the exit door, when Chico passed in front of her, just as the journalist thought: "What a phenomenon! An exemplary figure, a true lighthouse for humanity. Too bad he's homosexual."

We are reporting here simply the journalist's statement, whose name we are omitting for ethical reasons. Questions regarding the sexual orientation of others deserve great respect from us. We must remove ourselves from any prejudice or judgment.

Chico stopped in front of the journalist and said to her: "I am not what you are thinking. I have never had sexual relations with a woman, rather, with a man."

Many of those present did not understand this; but, later, the reporter told us what she had been thinking about the medium.

BIBLIOGRAPHICAL REFERENCES FOR RESEARCH

Scientists develop a technique to "read" thoughts.

Analyzing brain waves, a computer program was able to "guess" words that patients were thinking. American scientists created a method to discover words that patients were thinking, based on their brain waves. The technique, described in the scientific journal PLOS Biology, uses electrical signals from patients brains who were hearing different words. A computer was later capable of reconstructing sounds that the patients were thinking.

According to researchers, the method could be used in the future to help patients communicate if in a coma or with incarceration syndrome to communicate.

Images and Sounds

Recent studies have been perfecting ways to read thoughts. Last year, scientist Jack Gallant's team at the University of California, Berkeley, developed a way to relate patterns of blood flow in the brain to certain images that patients were thinking about.

Now, Brian Pasley of the same university has led a research project applying similar principles to sounds. His team concentrated on the Upper Temporal Lobe (UTL), a region of the brain that is not only part of the auditory mechanism, but also helps us to linguistically understand the sounds we hear.

Secret Word

Researchers monitored the brain waves of fifteen patients selected for surgery for epilepsy or tumors, while different loudspeakers played recordings of words and phrases. They then used a computer program to map the parts of the brain that reacted when the person heard different sound frequencies.

Afterward, the patients received a list of words and they chose one to think about. With the help of the computer program, the team was able to discover the patient's word.

They were even able to reconstruct some of the words, transforming brain waves into sounds, based on the computer's readings.

"This work has a dual nature: the first is the basic science of understanding how the brain works; the other takes a prosthetic point of view. People who have speech problems could use a prosthetic device when they are not able to speak, but can think about what they want to say," explained one of the authors of the study, Robert Knight.

"Patients then are giving us this information, so that it would be good for us to be able to give something in return to them."

The scientists explain, in the meantime, that the idea of "reading thoughts" still must be greatly perfected so that devices of that type can become a reality.

Globo.com – Ciência e Saúde – BBC Brasil. Published on 2/1/2012.

Chapter 6

Reading Thoughts and Mental Responses

If there was one particular talent of Chico's that most impressed me, it was undoubtedly his ability to read thoughts. Many cases of this are documented in biographical books about his mediumship, with examples of his work, humility, and charity.

In addition to the previously mentioned episode regarding Nosso Lar, there were two more events that surprised me.

One of them happened on a Saturday evening, after the Prayer Spiritist Group's meeting had ended but before Chico left. Chico insisted on saying goodbye to everyone there. Generally, the conversations were filled with teachings, and his giving autographs.

When the farewells were over, Chico was leaving, but was surrounded by a small crowd. I tried to get close enough to say goodbye because I was returning to São Paulo the next day, but there were too many people in the way.

At that moment, I thought: "I spent several days in contact with Chico, so it's a shame not to be able to say goodbye. But this crowd needs his contact more than I do. This is good for people, some of whom are very needy. So I left and headed to the car, a few blocks away, with some friends from the Home Workshop. Someone came running after us, calling out my name.

"Umberto, Umberto. Please, come back to the Center because Chico wants to say good-bye to you." To use a common expression, 'you could have knocked me over with a feather' from surprise. How come? He hadn't even seen me. How did he know that I had tried to approach him to take my leave?

I went back to the Center. Chico was waiting for me, standing near his car. As I approached, he said: "I didn't want you to go back to São Paulo without my saying good-bye to you."

Jesus! He had picked up my thoughts when I tried to approach him. This really impressed me.

On another occasion, I was at his house in the sitting room. It was Friday, around one o'clock in the morning, and several people were pressed against the window outside, and the room was full of young people from the São Paulo center. They began to ask questions about the book Libertação by André Luiz. He answered with great simplicity, and a certain amount of tact. Then I wanted to ask him a question about the oval shapes that André writes about in the book. I wanted him to talk a little more about Chapter 12, "At Margarida's House."

At that moment, he looked at me and smiled and then I heard his voice very clearly in my head say, "I can't talk about that now. Many of these young people are beginners in Spiritism, and such matters need to be covered with greater time so that they don't get incomplete information allowing for doubts. We'll talk later."

I had just witnessed another great experience. He not only read thoughts, but he also sent me an answer mentally. When I said I 'hear' his words, I did not mean that literally because the process occurred mentally. 'Telepathic transmission' is a more satisfactory description of this communication. I thought at the time, "There are lessons upon lessons.

With Chico, learning never stops."

BIBLIOGRAPHICAL REFERENCES FOR RESEARCH
Telepathy
... It is an exchange of impressions, consciously or unconsciously, between two centers of psychic activity.

Aksakof, Alexandre. *Animismo e Espiritismo,* **Trans. by Dr. C. S. 6**[th] **ed. Rio de Janeiro: FEB, 2002. 2 v. , C, Chapter 3.** [*Animism and Spiritism*]

Telepathy is direct communication, without any intermediaries, from one mind to another. According to some authors, a number of different forms of telepathy occur: guessing someone else's thought who is not participating in the experience; transmission of thought when two people are participating, transmitting, and receiving; when one influences another's mind (TS – telepathic suggestion); and when one exercises domination of another's mind (TH – telepathic hypnosis).

Barbosa, Pedro Franco. *Espiritismo Básico (Psicologia, Parapsicologia e Espiritismo).* **5**[th] **ed. Rio de Janeiro: FEB, 2002.** [*Basic Spiritism (Psychology, Parapsychology and Spiritism)*]

Telepathy becomes evident, which is nothing

more than a mental conversation from one being to another, crossing sidereal abysses and conquering overwhelming difficulties, thus overcoming, for the person who practices it, the barriers of materiality that intercept or retard the vibrations, finally impelled by legitimate feeling, to reach the pinnacle of possibility.

Pereira, Yvonne A. *Nas Voragens do Pecado.* **Pelo By the Spirit Charles. 10th ed. Rio de Janeiro: FEB, 2003.** [*In the Whirlpools of Sin*]

Chapter 7

Fluidified Water in the Gospel at Home

One of the interesting things about the Gospel at Home meeting, is the fluidification of water. After the Gospel meeting, there are many reports of water appearing with altered smell or appearance, with a variety of perfumes, flowers, or medication, or even different colors and textures. One such experience happened the first time that we took a bottle of water to be fluidified at a Gospel at Home meeting at Chico's house. At the end of the meeting, the water was full of little bright golden spheres which were slowly dissolving. Because Chico is a medium of ectoplasm, the waters he fluidified had a very special characteristic.

This occurs because the mentors can manipulate

the most subtle of fluids, spiritual ones or even the ectoplasm supplied by the medium, enriching water with perfumes or curative therapeutic agents. It should be remembered that we must not replace medications with fluidified water, but we can use it as a supplement.

These Gospel at Home meetings at Chico's house bought other surprises. At one meeting, the water smelled like roses, at another, like jasmine, or a mixture of essences, a great variety of perfumes and colors. We were impressed by the fact that fluidified water must be diluted at an average rate of five parts of regular water to one of fluidified water, since it was impossible to drink it straight after fluidification. The amount of perfumed fluids was so great that, if not diluted, it would burn the throat.

However, there is something more important than the phenomena of material transformation at Gospel meetings. It is the spiritual transformations of the human soul, which when touched, motivated, and oriented by the Good News of Jesus, undergoes the metamorphosis of love. And without any doubt, Chico did this with skill, helping us by his example of living the Master's Gospel.

More than the bubbling of waters, Chico put in

our hearts the effervescent joy of friendship, affection, and respect that come about from true love.

BIBLIOGRAPHICAL REFERENCES FOR RESEARCH
Water

Water, in view of its molecular structure, is an element that absorbs and conducts the bioenergy which is ministered to it. When magnetized and swallowed, it produces organic effects compatible with the fluid of which it is a carrier.

Franco, Divaldo P. *Loucura e Obsessão.* **By the Spirit Manoel P. de Miranda. 9th ed. Rio de Janeiro: FEB, 2003. Chapter 3.** [*Madness and Obsession*]

… water is the agent of nature that most quickly and completely absorbs fluids. Thus, the great therapeutic value of magnetized water, both for internal disorders and external ones.

Michaellus. *Magnetismo Espiritual.* **9th ed. Rio de Janeiro: FEB, 2005.** [*Spiritual Magnetism*]

… water absorbs the spiritual characteristics of the people in every home it touches… water doesn't just carry away waste material; it becomes filled with mental vibrations, too… water may be noxious in base hands, but healing when in the service of generous minds.

Pure water, as it moves, spreads the blessings of life; it carries away human thoughts of bitterness, hatred, and worry. All of this, in addition to its ordinary functions of keeping the body and home clean. And in that way it does the work of Divine Providence.

Xavier, Francisco Cândido. *Nosso Lar.* By the Spirit André Luiz. Anon. trans into English. Philadelphia: Allan Kardec Educational Society, 2000. P. 55.

Fluidified Water

Fluidification of water must always be done in an environment dedicated to prayer, in a reserved place properly prepared for the purpose. This fluidification may be done spiritually or through an incarnate prayer giver. In spiritual fluidification the recipient of water is simply put on a table or any other piece of furniture, in an atmosphere in which one page of the Gospel is read, followed by a prayer in which the Superior Spirits are asked to fluidify that water, always telling the purpose for which it is intended.

Gibier, Dr. Paul. *O Espiritismo; Faquirismo Oriental: Estudo Histórico Crítico, Experimental.* 5th ed. Rio de Janeiro: FEB, 2002. Chapter 2. [*Spiritism; Oriental Fakirism: Historical, Critical, Ex-

perimental Study]

... Water to which high-value magnetic resources have been added for the psychophysical equilibrium of those nearby ...

By the intermediation of fluidified water ... a precious force of medication can be carried out. There are injuries and deficiencies in the spiritual vehicle to be stamped on the physical body, which only magnetic intervention can alleviate, until those involved can receive the proper cure.

Xavier, Francisco Cândido. *Nos Domínios da Mediunidade.* **By the Spirit André Luiz. 32nd ed. Rio de Janeiro: FEB, 2005. Chapter 12. [*In the Domains of Mediumship*]**

Ectoplasm

Ectoplasm is the name that is given to the fluid of a psychosomatic nature, coming from mediums of materialization and which the spirits use to become visible and tangible to the eyes and the touch of humans.

Anjos, Luciano dos; Miranda, Hermínio C. *Crônicas de Um e de Outro: de Kennedy ao Homem Artificial.* **Preface by Abelardo Idalgo Magalhães. Rio de Janeiro: FEB, 1975.** [*Chronicles of One and Another: From Kennedy to the Artificial Man*]

... it is, in its essence, a physiological prolongation of the medium. It is an intimate, live substance, a component of the human being, extremely sensitive, moist, sticky, viscous, slightly grayish (presently, we know that the whiteness of this material is unstable, depending almost always on the evolutionary state of the entity; in modern language, it is the biological plasma that makes up the creature.) ...

Imbassahy, Carlos. À Margem do Espiritismo: Refutação à Crítica Feita à Parte Filosófica do Espiritismo. Preface by Guillon Ribeiro. 4th ed. Rio de Janeiro; FEB, 2002. [*At the Edge of Spiritism: Refutation to Criticism Made Against the Philosophical Part of Spiritism*]

... a colorless [substance], slightly vaporous, fluid, without smell, traces of cellular waste and saliva. Whitish deposit. Slightly alkaline reaction...

With this complex substance, evidently emanated from the body of the medium and perhaps some of those surrounding him or her, discarnate spirits compose their tangible manifestations called materializations...

Miranda, Hermínio C. *Reencarnação e Imortalidade*. 5th ed. Rio de Janeiro: FEB, 2002. Chapter 14. [*Reincarnation and Immortality*]

This materializing force is like others manipulated in our tasks of interchange. It does not depend on the character and moral qualities of those who possess it, constituting emanations from the psychophysical world, of which cytoplasm is one of the sources. In some rare individuals, we find similar energy with a higher percentage of exteriorization; however, we know that it will be of a more abundant future and more easily approached, when the human collectivity reaches a high level of maturity ... There we have the light and plastic material that we need for materialization. We can divide it into three essential elements... that is - A fluids, representing the superior and subtle forces of our sphere; B fluids, defining the resources of the medium and the companions that assist him or her; and C fluids, constituting energies taken from terrestrial nature. A Fluids may be the most pure and C fluids may be the most docile; however, B fluids, born of the action of incarnate companions and, very notably, the medium, are capable of ruining our most noble projects.

... Ectoplasm is situated between dense matter and perispirit matter... and is a resource to all forms of nature... It is an amorphous element, of great power and vitality. It may be compared to the genuine protoplasmic mass, and is extremely sensitive, animated by creative principles that function as conductors of electricity and magnetism, but which are invariably subordinate to the thought and will of the medium that exteriorizes it or of the discarnate spirit, or not, who tunes in to the mediunic mind, dominating its mode of being. It is infinitely plastic, of a partial or total form to the entities that make themselves visible to the eyes of earthly companions or before the photographic lens. It has the consistency of thread, or of a small stick or other type of formation. It may be visible or invisible, in the phenomenon of levitation, and makes substantial the images created by the imagination of the medium or of the companions who help in being mentally tuned in to him.

Xavier, Francisco Cândido. *Nos Domínios da Mediunidade.* **By the Spirit André Luiz. 32rd ed. Rio de Janeiro: FEB, 2005.** [*In the Domains of Mediumship*]

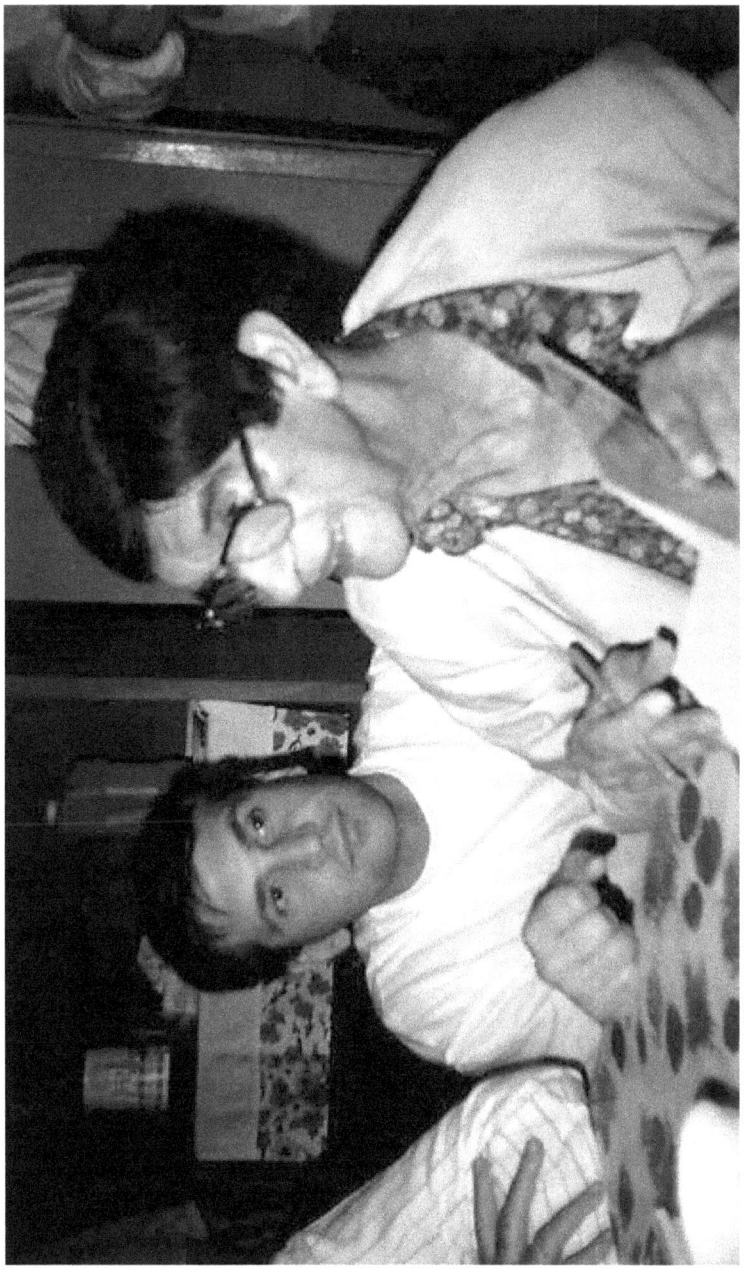

Umberto Fabbri and Chico Xavier

Chapter 8

Unexpected Visit

Some stories about Chico's life, as told by our leader Mrs. Yolanda Cezar, were spooky enough to make someone want to sleep with the lights on, which certainly occurred to a number of people who heard the stories at dawn. There is something to be said about Spiritists who are afraid of spirits.

Chico told us one such story to make your hair stand on end, even for those without hair. He told us that after he had just gone to bed, at about two in the morning, there appeared at the foot of his bed a being that was a mixture of man and monster. The entity was very malformed, which was the result of his immorality and lack of respect for himself and others.

This occurs when the creature possesses an inferior moral state, for not knowing, and not following,

Divine Laws, or even the will of the spirit. This lack of knowledge or obedience may give form to the perispirit. Generally, such spirits do this to terrify those that they wish to harm.

Well, let's go on with the story:

The spirit was tall, well over six feet, and his skin had a scaly covering, and his red eyes seemed to be injected with blood. He looked like a demon. That was scary! It asked Chico: "Why did you call me?" Chico did not answer, because he had not called anyone. Since the visitor received no answer, it asked again: "Why did you call me?" This was a mental or telepathic dialogue.

Chico thought: "My God, and now what? If I say that I called it, I have to give a reason; if I say I didn't call, it may be offended. Faced with such a dilemma, I thought it best to act with the greatest care and I responded:

"'I called you so you could bless me.' The entity, perplexed, turned and said:

"'Oh, Chico, you are hopeless!'

"And he went out the door…"

BIBLIOGRAPHICAL REFERENCES FOR RESEARCH
Ectoplasm

… Ectoplasm, that is, the projection of a force

outside the body of the medium, has the first phase of invisibility; a second one during which a vapor or a "fluidic" thread appears, which is when it begins to be visible; and a third phase during which it is tangible, visible, and sometimes without form...

Cerviño, Jayme. *Além do Inconsciente.* 5th ed. Rio de Janeiro: FEB, 2005. Chapter 3. [*Beyond the Unconscious*]

Perispirit

An essential part of the human complex, the perispirit or psychosoma is made up of various fluids that come together, resulting from the primitive universal energy of which each orb is composed, generating hyperphysical matter, which is transformed into a plastic mediator between the spirit and the body.

... A temporary covering, it is absolutely necessary for incarnation and reincarnation; it is just as dense or subtle as the evolution of the spirit with which it is involved.

... It is not a condensation of the electrical chaos or of magnetic forces; rather, it possesses its own malleable structure, under some circumstances tangible - like some materializations of discarnate souls, in the apparitions of the living and the dead - active in transportation and levitations; now ponderable, being able to increase or diminish the volume and weight of the body; now imponderable, as occurs in dematerializations and transfigurations.

... Since the appreciable lessons of Vedanta when Manu, Māyā, and Kosha appeared, it was known in esoteric Buddhism as Kama-rupa, while in Egyptian Eremitism it appeared in the quality of Kha, to advance, in the Hebraic Kabala as a manifestation of Rouach.

The Chinese, Greeks, and Romans had knowledge of its reality, and identified it. Pythagoras, more tuned in to metaphysical studies, called it subtle flesh of the soul, and Aristotle, in his study of the human soul, considered it a subtle and ethereal body. Aristotle was a materialist and did not believe in spirit; the Stoics taught this as well as Plato. The Neoplatonics from Alexandria, among them Origin who was the father of the Doctrine of Principles, identified it as 'the aura'. Tertullian, the giant inspired by the Apologetics, saw it as the vital body of the soul, while Proclus characterized it as the vehicle of the soul.

In modern culture, Paracelsus, in the 16th Century, detected it as an astral body, as shown by notable research done in the field of chemistry, as well as in parallel studies of medicine with philosophy. Following that, Leibniz replaced the pantheistic concepts of Spinoza, when he theorized that all matter consisted of spiritual atoms or 'monads', surprisingly naming it 'fluidic body'.

This is in perfect consonance with the latest discoveries, in the detection experiments by efluvoscopy and efluviography, (called the bioplasmic body). The Apostle Paul had already called it the spiritual body, as he wrote in Corinthians (First Epistle, 15:44), 'a corruptible body', and then later in the same Epistle, verse 53; or 'soul', in his letter to the Thessalonians (First Epistle 5:23), outliving death

Franco, Divaldo P. *Estudos Espíritas*. By the Spirit Joanna de Angelis. 7th ed. Rio de Janeiro: FEB, 1999. Chapter 7. [*Spiritist Studies*]

See also the bibliographic references of Chapter 7: "Fluidified Water in the Gospel at Home."

Chapter 9

The Snake Around the Neck

We know through Spiritist literature of various cases of deformation of the perispirit, caused by behavior in disharmony with Divine Laws. Some beings wasted their opportunities for growth, both in the reincarnation process and during the interval between reincarnations, utilizing their gifts to attack their neighbors cruelly, and disrespecting the basic right of others to live.

Such spirits create real, private hells for themselves, burning their insides. While suffering atrociously, when their conscience awakes they become the so-called "victims," in the obsessive processes of others who were accomplices to their crimes or who were their torture victims.

Being aggressors against themselves, such entities create great deformations in their perispirit that only Divine Grace can fix through reincarnation cycles, when they will have the opportunity for renewal by learning. Our brethren will have the tireless help of spiritual mentors always ready to give aid.

In another chapter, we mentioned the experience of our Chico with the frightening entity that appeared in his room. The medium has the faculty of ectoplasm, which may be utilized by enlightened spirits to care for those creatures in lamentable states, who need greater contact in the material field, in order to receive needed assistance.

We can make an analogy with the scuba diver who uses a diving suit, clothing that makes it possible for him to interact with elements of the sea. In the same way, in order to make themselves perceptible and have contact with the incarnate, for a great variety of needs, spirits use ectoplasm to clothe their perispirit with a more material substance, thus making it possible to contact the incarnate.

The following is one such example. It was late at night when Chico ended one of his psychographing sessions. After taking leave of all his visitors, he went into his room to get his necessary rest. He was alone that night. Suddenly, an entity almost completely materialized, resembling a snake or viper, having a face that was half human and half serpent with gigantic fangs, wrapped around the medium's body and holding its deformed 'face' just a few inches from Chico's face.

Chico told us this tale at two in the morning, and as Mrs. Yolanda said, it would be a night to sleep with the light on - that old cliché of Spiritists who are afraid of spirits.

I asked a question before Chico had time to tell the whole story: "So, Chico, what did you do then?"

"Me? At first I didn't do anything, because nothing like that had ever happened to me before. I felt the thing's breath in my face, it was so close to me."

Obviously, we all had our eyes popping out, burning with curiosity.

The medium continued: "I immediately said a prayer and in moments Emmanuel appeared."

Then someone said: "So, with Emmanuel was the situation was resolved? ."

"Not really," answered Chico. "Our mentors do not do the work for us. They help us, assist us, clarify things, enlighten, but the work is ours. Otherwise, where is the reward without effort? So Emmanuel turned to me and said, 'Chico, these our brethren need a lot of love. Only our vibrations of profound love can bring some peace and clarity to their tormented minds.'

"I began to vibrate a lot of love, encompassing that poor creature in much light, while it continued to squeeze me with its body wrapped around mine, exhaling its stinky hot breath onto my face. That was when, after several minutes, I began to feel the pressure reduce and, little by little, the entity was calming down, and finally, it let go of me and went slithering away just like a snake. I prayed a lot for it, even after it left, asking God and Jesus to surround it with grace and love."

A colleague in the group said: "Chico, if it had happened to me, I would have disincarnated from freight."

We all had a good laugh.

BIOGRAPHICAL REFERENCES FOR RESEARCH

In Chapter 7, "Fluidified Water in the Gospel at Home" and in Chapter 3, "Unexpected Visit," we inserted items that refer to ectoplasm.

In order to avoid being repetitive, we include here references to two works about vibrations of

love, in favor of one's neighbor, as well as examples of deformations of the perispirit, specifically in the case of ovoids.

Vibration

… vibrations of fraternal love, which Christ left for us, are real energies that dissolve vengeance, persecution, lack of discipline, vanity, and selfishness that have tormented the human experience.

Xavier, Francisco Cândido. *Libertação*. By the Spirit André Luiz. 29th ed. Rio de Janeiro: FEB, 2005. [*Liberation*]

The incarnate … still do not know how to help us (the discarnate), harmonically through mental emissions (vibrations).

Xavier, Francisco Cândido. *Missionários da Luz*. By the Spirit André Luiz. 39th ed. Rio de Janeiro: FEB, 2004. [*Missionaries of Light*]

Ovoid

… Ovoids are live spheroids, sad human minds without capacity for manifestation…

Xavier, Francisco Cândido. *Libertação* [op. cit.] Chapter 6 [*Liberation*]

Finding himself to be in a climate adverse to his mode of being, primitive man, becoming detached from the physical shell, refuses to move to the extra-physical sphere, slowly becoming submerged in the atrophy of the cells that weave his spiritual body, through self-hypnotizing monoideism, caused by fixed, depressive thought that defines his anxiety to return to the physiological shelter. In this period, we habitually affirm that the discarnate soul has lost his spiritual body, transubstantiating into an ovoid body, something that occurs, however, with numerous discarnate spirits in states of imbalance. We should note that this form, according to our ritual of perception, expresses the mental body of individuality, closing in upon itself, according to the ontogenetic principles of Divine Creation; all of the virtual organs of exteriorization of the soul, in terrestrial and spiritual circles, just like the apparently simple egg, today contain the powerful bird of tomorrow, or like the tiny seed, which contains all of the embryonic fabric of the vigorous tree that it will become in the future.

Xavier, Francisco Cândido. *Evolução em Dois Mundos.* **By the Spirit André Luiz. 23rd ed. Rio de Janeiro: FEB, 2005. (Part I, Chapter 12).** [*Evolution on Two Worlds*]

Innumerable unfortunate ones, stubbornly taking justice into their own hands, or entrusting vicious desires, when freed from the physical vehicle, subtly involve those who make them the object of calculated attention. Self-hypnotized by images of affectivity or revenge, infinitely repeated by themselves, they end up in a deplorable monoideistic fixation, beyond the notions of space and time, showing, step by step, enormous changes in the morphology of the spiritual vehicle, such that the psychosomatic organs are restricted for lack of use. They are similar to ovoids, tied to the victims themselves who, in general, mechanically accept the influence, in the face of later thoughts of remorse or sorrow, of voracious hate or demanding egotism, which feed on the brain itself, through incessant mental waves.

Ibid. **(part I, Chapter 15).**

Chapter 10

A Spirit in Need

Sometimes I commented, with friends from the Home Workshop, on my impression that we were experiencing moments in another dimension while we were in Chico's presence. The world from his side made possible experiences that constantly confirmed the existence of the spiritual realm and of spirituality and its interactions with us.

The mediunic episodes were so many and so routine, and treated by Chico with extreme naturalness that enchanted us.

In one of our bimonthly visits, we found that the medium, to our surprise, had part of his face scratched and bruised. Without our asking him about it, he read our thoughts, and narrated this tale, starting simply:

"Don't be worried. I'm fine, in spite of the bruises and a few scratches. There was a man in our house who wanted to talk about his son who had disincarnated a few days before. I noticed that he was accompanied by the discarnate son. The son appeared extremely needy, caused by his emotional maladjustment before his death. He was not aware of his own spiritual state. I could see that his case was very serious and I recommended that we help him at the Prayer Spiritual Group, later that same night."

Chico then described his observations.

"Poor boy, he was frightened by the presence of his spiritual friends who were there to help him. Because of his imbalance, he felt threatened by his friends. In desperation, he tried to flee and lost control, throwing himself to the ground."

We were amazed at the story that Chico was telling us, not only because of the condition of the discarnate boy, but also because of his mediunic capacity, primarily his ectoplasm that made such unusual events possible on the physical plane.

The young man was cared for and healed by his spiritual friends, and was carried to a special place for treatment on the spiritual plane.

This was one more unforgettable lesson for all those

present. Later on, we discussed how much we would still have to study to understand mediumship and all of its nuance.

BIBLIOGRAPHICAL REFERENCES FOR RESEARCH
Spirits that are unaware of their own situation
They are not aware that they are on the spiritual plane. They do not know that they have died and they feel attracted to the places where they lived, or where the center of their interest lies.

Schubert, Suely Caldas. *Obsessão/Desobsessão: Profilaxia e Terapêutica Espíritas*. 16th ed. Rio de Janeiro: FEB, 2004. [*Obsession/Disobsession: Spiritist Prophylaxis and Therapy*]

Suffering Spirits
Those spirits, perturbed by death, still believe for some time that they belong to earthly life. Their gross fluids do not allow them to enter into a relationship with more advanced spirits, so that they are taken to study groups to be instructed about their new condition.

... they are companions that still have their minds in a vibratory context identical to that of their existence in the flesh. In the stage which they are going through, they are helped more quickly with the aid of the incarnate, because they are still breathing in that band of impressions.

Peralva, Martins. *Mediunidade e Evolução.* 5th ed. Rio de Janeiro: FEB, 1987. [*Mediumship and Evolution*]

Ectoplasm

See the bibliographical references for Chapter 7: "Fluidified Water in the Gospel at Home."

Chapter 11

Gospel in the Pocket

Enormous lines were forming after Saturday night's work at the Prayer Spiritist Group. Everyone wanted to say good-bye to Chico, shake his hand, exchange a kiss with him, and hear words of encouragement and inspiration.

"Uncle" Pedro, as he was known, helped keep the line moving along because the people in front of Chico would not let go of his hand. Everyone wanted to stay a little longer for one more word, one more photograph. It was very common for people of all ages and sexes to exchange kisses on the face with Chico. Some kissed his hands and Chico immediately repeated the gesture, and would kiss their hands, others on the face, and the medium always responded in kind.

One Saturday night, there was a distinct gentleman wearing a coat and tie, who was in line and was watching everything with great attention. The conversations, the kisses... When he reached the medium, Chico asked him:

"Did you enjoy our meeting?"

"Yes, Chico. I found everything very instructive and interesting, but I have a comment, if you will allow me, about its end."

"Of course, please make your comment," said Chico.

"I liked everything, but this business of people staying to kiss you and you kissing them back: if you'll pardon me, but I think this is a bit too much..."

Chico said very simply: "Please excuse us if this bothers you, but Emmanuel is here at our side, and he is asking you to get out the Gospel in your coat's right inside pocket and open to Matthew, Chapter 12, Verse 34, and read to us."

"... for out of the abundance of the heart the mouth speaketh"

Further comments are totally unnecessary, is that not so?

Emmanuel: Spiritual mentor of Chico. The stress is

on our to speaking a little about the medium's ability as a seer. It is known that his ability to see spirits was so strong that at times Chico would fail to note the difference between the incarnate and the discarnate, such was the clarity with which he saw the spirits.

BIBLIOGRAPHICAL REFERENCES FOR RESEARCH

Evil speaking

Evil speaking is the act of speaking ill of people ... It is more terrible than physical aggression. Much more than the body, it wounds human dignity, soils reputations, and destroys existences.

Simonetti, Richard. *A Voz do Monte.* 7th **ed. Rio de Janeiro: FEB, 2003.** [*Voice from the Mount*]

Speaking ill, in its legitimate meaning, would be to indulge inferior instincts and renounce our divine cooperation with God, becoming a critic of His works.

Xavier, Francisco Cândido. *Fonte Viva.* **By the Spirit Emmanuel. 33rd ed. Rio de Janeiro: FEB, 2005.** [*Live Fountain*]

Evil Speaker

An evil speaker is a tormented soul who debates in the torrents of his own inferiority. His vision is taken over and he sees everything through the heavy lenses that he wears.

Franco, Divaldo P. *Lampadário Espírita*. **By the Spirit Joanna de Ângelis. 7**th **ed. , Rio de Janeiro: FEB, 2005.** [*Spiritist Lamppost*]

See also references in Chapter 33, "Paul and Steven: A Seer and Hearer Medium."

Chapter 12

Trial or Atonement?

It is common when we look at difficult situations to ask: "Is this a trial or an atonement?" As if the Laws of God only presented two circumstances, without variables of any kind.

As we said earlier, the line that formed with people who wanted to say good-bye to Chico was enormous. We have memories of great lessons picked up at those moments.

It was dawn on a Saturday when a middle-aged woman was in the line, who looked poor, carrying on her shoulders a teenage boy as if he were a backpack. She was very poor, and not having enough money for a wheelchair, she carried that child as well as she could, greatly stirring us. The boy was very short, because he was a tetraplegic, with complete congenital visual and mental deficiencies.

That poor mother, approaching "Uncle Chico," asked him to bless her son...

Chico said a prayer, laying his hands on the boy's head, and handed the poor woman the small amount of money he had in his pocket. As she was leaving, Chico mentally asked the spirit of Dr. Bezerra de Menezes what that boy's spirit had done to reincarnate in such a difficult situation.

The answer was: "Chico, he didn't do anything needing atonement, as we usually understand it. He asked to come like that with his body totally compromised."

"And Dr. Bezerra, could you give the reason for that request?"

"Of course, Chico. The spirit in question, over his past five lives, brought about his departure from his body by suicide. Every time he faced a serious problem, in these past lives, he would commit suicide. Thus a vicious cycle would start in relation to disincaration, when the automation of violent departure from the physical body became hardened in his psyche.

"In order for him to break this cycle, he asked Divine Mercy and the mentors in charge of his reincarnation to let him return to the planet with his body totally disabled so that he would reach the end of his life by natural means, being unable to violently impose the process upon himself.

"In this way, he would reinstate the natural process of death in his psyche, putting him on the necessary path for his transformation and growth."

To conclude the narrative, Chico told us:

"See how the mercy and the love of God always work for our readjustment. A victim of suicide, before being punished, is the son or daughter who most needs attention."

BIBLIOGRAPHICAL REFERENCES FOR RESEARCH

Trial or Atonement: We also recommend reading Chapter 24, "Different Stories, but with the Same Ending."

Suicide

A person who commits suicide is the first and greatest victim of his own deception. He kills himself to flee from his problems, his pains, and his afflictions, and as soon as he recovers, on the other side of life, he will have sufficient lucidity to understand his new situation and will discover, profoundly anguished, that he did not succeed in fleeing from himself, nor from his sufferings. He changed his position in life, he exchanged one series of pains for others that are even more afflictive, more terrible, and more dramatic.

In a childish attempt to slip by some Divine Laws, he violated other even more serious ones that demand the most painful reparations.

Anjos, Luciano dos, Miranda, Hermínio C. *Crônicas de Um e de Outro: De Kennedy ao Homem Artificial.* Rio de Janeiro: FEB, 1975. [*Chronicles of One and Another: From Kennedy to the Artificial Man*]

Suicide is the culmination of a state of alienation that begins subtly. The candidate does not think in a balanced way; he does not realize the suffering that his act gives to those who love him. Because he loses the capacity of discernment, he considers it the only solution, forgetting that time always resolves all problems, rather than causing them. His anxious haste to flee and the despair inside him push the sick person into an exit with no return.

Franco, Divaldo P. *Loucura e Obsessão.* By the Spirit Manoel P. de Miranda. 9th ed. , Rio de Janeiro: FEB, 2003. [*Madness and Obsession*]

Suicide is a terrible evil that is increasing among

humankind and which must be fought against by all men. This mental rigidity that solves things with a tragic solution is a complex disease.

To make all people aware of the consequences of the act, in the other world, in the pains that are caused to family members, and in the violation of Divine Laws, is the healthy way to reduce occurrences of this insolvable solution. To maintain a dialog with goodness and patience with people who have a tendency toward suicide; to suggest that they give themselves a little more time while their problems may change; to avoid offering illusory bases for fleeting hopes that time will destroy; to stimulate personal worth; to light a light in the tunnel of despair, among other things, constitute preventive therapy, which will be strengthened by the exercise of prayer, optimistic spiritual readings, blessings, and the use of fluidified water.

Franco, Divaldo P. *Temas da Vida e da Morte.* **By the Spirit Manoel P. de Miranda. 5th ed. Rio de Janeiro: FEB, 2005.** [*Topics of Life and Death*]

Helpful pain

... by means of the intercession of friends devoted to our happiness and our victory, we receive the blessing of prolonged and painful infirmities in the physical shell, whether to prevent our falling into a criminal abyss, or, more often, to prepare us for the process of disincarnation, so that we will not be taken by sudden surprise in the transition to death. A heart attack, thrombosis, paralysis, long-lasting cancer, early senility, and other calamities of organic life sometimes constitute helpful pains so that the soul can recover from certain deceptions that it has fallen into during the existence of the dense body, rehabilitating it through long reflections and beneficial discipline, for the respectable entry into spiritual life.

Xavier, Francisco Cândido. *Ação e Reação.* **By the Spirit André Luiz. 26th ed. Rio de Janeiro: FEB, 2004.** [*Action and Reaction*]

Chapter 13

Food for the Cats

As we have mentioned before, In the Prayer Spiritist Group there was a long line to greet Chico after the night's work. It was always a great opportunity for everyone to learn; the medium would give unforgettable lessons. After one meeting when the greeting line was enormous, getting into the wee hours of dawn, a woman commented to Chico when saying good-bye to him:

"Chico, you have a lot of cats, don't you?"

"Yes, sister, I have a few."

"Can you believe, Chico, that I am receiving recipes for cat food through mediumship?"

It matters little whether the recipes were coming through mediumship or through animals. What would be really important was the lesson in patience that some people would glean.

One of my friends from the Home Workshop group, who was in the line and close to the scene, would later declare:

"My gosh! Chico has so many people to see and they are taking his time up with this kind of thing. Cat food recipes received through mediumship! Come on, give me a break!"

"Better not to think that way," he declared. "If regret killed..."

"I missed nothing because Chico took the woman's hand and said:

"'You don't say! Recipes for cat food? How marvelous! Do you happen to have one with you?'

"'I do, Chico, several.'

"'Well, I would love to see them and copy one or two.' Saying that, Chico looked over at our colleague and give a little smile."

Our companion said to us:

"I could have died! He had read my thoughts and I had no place to hide.

BIBLIOGRAPHICAL REFERENCES FOR RESEARCH
Patience
Pain is a blessing sent by God to all His elected;

so, when you suffer, do not allow yourself to become afflicted; rather bless the Omnipotent Who, through the pain of this world, has chosen you to receive glory in Heaven.

Be patient, because this is also a charity; everyone should practice the law of charity as taught by Christ, Who is God's Envoy. Charity given to the poor in the form of alms is the easiest of all. However, there is another kind of charity which is much more laborious and so consequently offers higher merit. That is to forgive all those placed in your pathway by God to act as instruments for your suffering and to test your patience.

We know full well that life is difficult, being composed of so many apparently useless, insignificant and valueless things which act as repeated pinpricks and end up hurting us. However, if on the one hand we observe with care the duties imposed upon us, and on the other recognise the consolations and compensations received, then we must admit that the blessings are far more numerous than the pains.
When our eyes are raised up to Heaven our burdens appear to be less heavy than when our brow is bowed down to the earth.

Courage, my friends! Christ is your model. He

suffered far more than any of you and had nothing to offer penitence for, whereas we must atone for our past and thereby fortify ourselves for the future. So be patient; be Christians! This word summarizes everything.

A Friendly Spirit (Le Havre, 1862)

Kardec, Allan. *The Gospel According to Spiritism.* **English trans. by J. A. Duncan. London: The Headquarters Publishing Co Ltd, 1987. Pp. 101.**

Also see Chapter 6: "Reading Thoughts and Mental Responses."

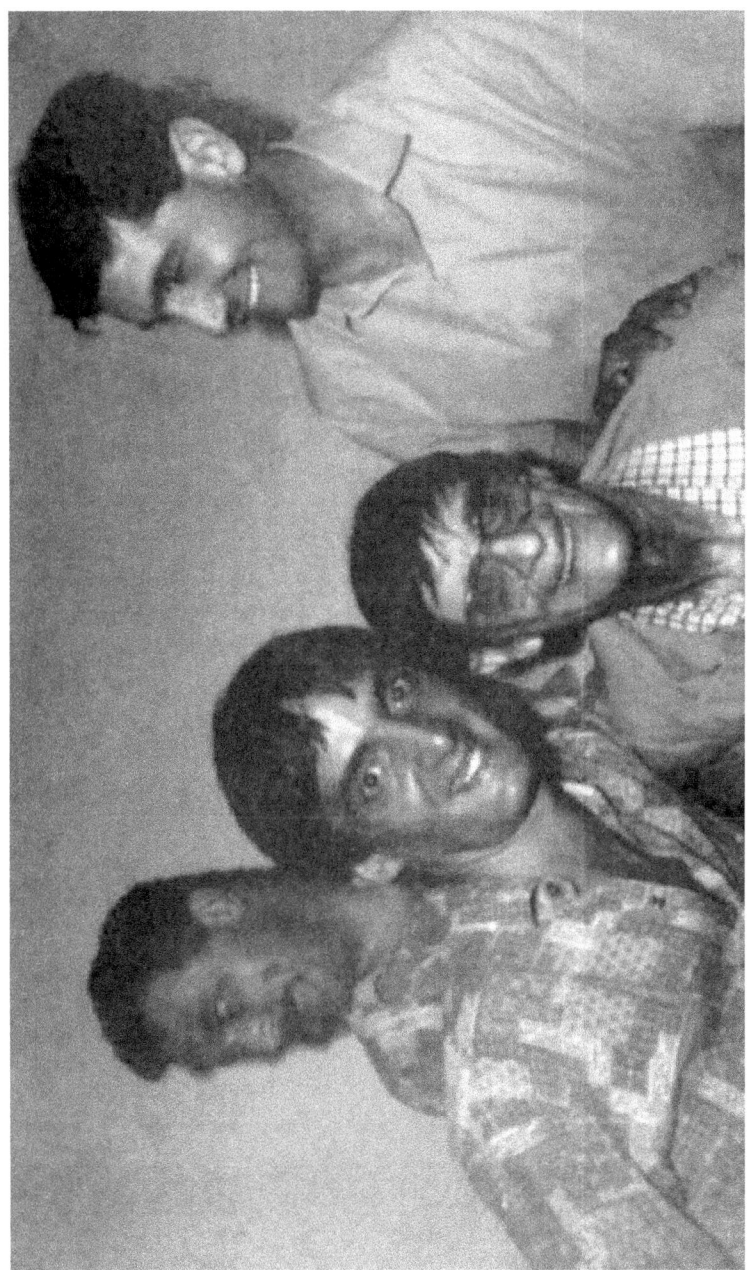

Eliomar, Chico Xavier, Umberto Fabbri and Mauro in the back

Chapter 14

The Line

As we have said, the lines at the Prayer Spiritist Group taught us a lot of lessons. We were impressed by the attention that Chico gave to the people who approached him. With great respect and sensitivity he would talk in detail about the things that brought his worried guests to the Center.

There was one very interesting episode; I have changed the names for ethical reasons. A couple, Sérgio and Dulce Almeida, were visiting the Prayer Spiritist Center for the first time. They had been born to Catholic families, and had five children, four girls and one boy. The boy, named Roberto, had been preparing to take on the father's business, who at the time was an important businessman in São Paulo.

Roberto was at the peak of his youth, 22 years old. He was athletic, intelligent, well prepared, and about to complete his prestigious academic training, when he suddenly disincarnated.

His death occurred at a beach on the São Paulo coastline. He went to sleep under a scalding sun. When he awoke he felt hot and so went to the sea to cool off. As he put his feet in the cold sea water, he had thermal shock, which brought about an immediate myocardial attack. The desolate family was looking for an explanation for the tragedy and had decided to seek out the medium from Uberaba.

There was no lack of surprise at the first meeting. The couple was in line to be attended to by Chico when the medium approached them and asked: "How are Sérgio and Dulce Almeida getting along?" Both of them were stupefied by the question. How could Chico know their names without any introduction or prior contact?

The surprises continued coming, because Chico asked them further:

"How are your daughters doing, A, B, C and D? Are they all well? I see that they were not able to come with you because of school, since classes are in session. They are very studious and they are taking care of your home at street Desembargador do Valle, 333, in neighborhood X, with great care and affection, like the good daughters that they are.

"Our Roberto (the boy who had passed away) asked me to tell you that he is very well, and he is missing his beloved parents and sisters, but he has received a great deal of support from his grandparents: Dorival and Carmen Almeida. They greeted him on the spiritual plane, with hearts full of love, which is a blessed support for his longing for everyone, especially his loving mother.

"He also tells us that it is possible, with authorization from the noble mentors that accompany him, to try, to try, given the great emotion that it involves, to put on paper some lines through our intermediary at the meeting tonight.

"Don't worry any more about the condition of our Roberto, because it is the best possible, and God, who loves us, being our Father, never fails to give us support. Until later tonight, then."

We can find some explanations about our Chico's mediumship, in the work of André Luiz, psychographed by Chico himself, entitled Nos Domínios da Mediunidade, Chapter 16 – "Mediunic Mandate."

BIBLIOGRAPHICAL REFERENCES FOR RESEARCH
Mediunic Mandate

It was almost eight o'clock when we stopped in front of the somber building, surrounded by a number of vehicles. Many people were going and coming. Discarnate spirits, in great numbers, were congregating inside the building and outside it. Aware of our plan, they stretched out attentively, blocking access of impenitent or mocking spirits.

Different groups of people gained entrance to the house, but at the entrance they experienced the separation of certain spirits who were following them, spirits that were not simply curious or sufferers, but rather blasphemers dedicated to evil.

These cases, however, were the exception, because, in general, the discarnate brothers and sisters were suffering and infirm, as much in need of brotherly help as the ill and afflicted who were accompanying us.

We entered. A great table in the center of the vast room was surrounded by a long and shiny isolation rope. At the back there was a spacious area reserved for those who needed assistance, incarnate or not; this area was also protected by magnetic lines of defense, under the careful eye of guards who belong to our sphere of action.

At the front, across from the entrance, various spiritual benefactors were talking among themselves, and next to them, a respectable lady was listening helpfully to several patients. The matron appeared covered by an extensive halo of opaline radiation, and, no matter how hard the projectors of somber substance tried to get to her, through the solicitations of the suffers who were addressing her, she maintained her own always lucid aura, not allowing the emissions of sickly fluids to reach her energy field.

Pointing at her with his left hand, the Assistant told us:

"She is our Sister Ambrosina, who, for more than twenty years , has tried to bring to Christian mediumship the best she possesses. For love of the ideal that guides us, she renounced the pleasures of the world, including the greatest comfort of the domestic sanctuary, since she spent her youth working, without the consolation of marriage." Ambrosina had a jagged, wrinkled face, reflecting, nonetheless, the peace that vibrated within her being. On her head, among her grey hairs, a little funnel of light was evident, like a delicate adornment.

Intrigued, we consulted the experience of our guide

and he immediately explained:

"It is an ultra-sensitive magnetic device, through which the medium lives in constant contact with the person responsible for the spiritual work that she does. For the time she has put into the cause for good and for the sacrifices which she has made, Ambrosina received from the Superior Plane a mandate for mediunic service, meriting, for this reason, the most intimate association with the instructor who directs the tasks. Having grown in influence, she found herself overwhelmed by requests from multiple centers. Inspiring faith and hope in all those who approach the priesthood of fraternity and comprehension, she is naturally harassed by the most disconcerting appeals.

"So her life is overwhelmed by requests and supplications?" asked Hilário, always curious.

"Up to a certain point, yes, because she symbolizes a bridge between two worlds; however, with evangelic patience, she knows how to help others so they can help each other, because it would not be possible for her to find solutions for all of the problems brought to her."

We approached the good, modest medium and we saw that she was thoughtful, in spite of the stifled murmuring around her. Not far away, the combined thinking of two people revealed lamentable crime scenes in which they had been involved. And, as Mrs. Ambrosina perceived them, she reflected, speaking without words audible only to us: "Beloved spiritual friends, what is there to do? I identify our delinquent brothers and I recognize their commitments... A man was eliminated... I see the agony portrayed in the memories of those responsible... What are our unfortunate companions looking for here, as they have fled from terrestrial justice?"

Then we noticed that the medium was afraid of losing the vibratory harmony that was particular to her. She did not desire to become absorbed in any conversation about the aforementioned visitors. That was when one of the mentors present approached her and calmed her down:

"Ambrosina, don't be fearful. Calm down. We need not let affliction disturb us. Get used to seeing our unfortunate brethren in that pitiable state. Remember that we are here to help, and that remedies are not for the healthy. Have compassion, keep your own balance. We owe love and respect to each other and, the more unfortunate people are, the more help they need. It is essential that we receive our brothers who are committed to evil, like the ill who seek affection."

The medium calmed down. She continued to talk naturally with the other visitors. Here, someone wanted healing for a tormented heart or asked for help for less fortunate relatives. There, fraternal assistance was sought for desperately sick loved ones.

Mrs. Ambrosina consoled and promised, "When Gabriel, the leader, arrives, the matter will be explained to you. Certainly, he will bring the necessary aid."

Not much later, Gabriel, the highest-ranking mentor of the house, came into the room, accompanied by a large group of friends. They settled themselves in intimate conversation at the front of the table. The entities there at the meeting with the most noble mental life established a wide beam of light to block the shadows that subjugated most of the souls, both incarnate and discarnate.

Gabriel and his assistants embraced us generously. We shared a wonderful happiness, so great was the jubilation of the instructors and spiritual workers. Despite having to treat the ill and suffering on both planes, that did not diminish their hope, peace, and optimism... They were all there with their selfless and learned leader, to whom Áulus did not withhold his commendation, along with physicians, professors, nurses, and discarnate helpers, ready to serve in the good work.

They radiated such beauty and happiness that Hilário, just as overwhelmed as I, began asking eager questions. 'Could those friends - considering the messages of light and sympathy that they projected of themselves - could they be the high ambassadors of Divine Providence? ' 'Did they perhaps enjoy the company of the saints?' 'Could they live in personal communion with Christ? ' 'Could they have reached the position of impeccable beings? '

The Assistant smiled good-naturedly and explained:

"Nothing like that. With all of the veneration that we owe them, we must think of them as vanguards of progress, but not infallible. They are great souls in a blessed process of sublimation, deserving of our reverence for the degree of elevation that they have achieved. Nonetheless, they are spirits still linked to earthly humanity, and in whose breast they will take more souls, through reincarnation, to accomplish valuable work.

"In the meantime, in this assembly of tortured spirits, are they so enlightened that they are free from error?"

"No," responded Áulus, understandingly. "We cannot demand qualities that only apply to spirits that have reached absolute sublimation. They are exponents of brotherhood and superior knowledge; however, they still have the capacity to make mistakes. They excel in good will, in culture, and in their self-sacrifice while helping their reincarnated companions, but they can make mistakes, which they quickly attempt to correct without the vanity that often hampers people on earth. Here we have, for example, various physicians without the constraints of physical experience. In spite of being excellent workers, dedicated and well-meaning in the mission that they are performing, it would not be permissible, however, for them to be promoted from one moment to the next, from the fragmentary science of the world to full knowledge. With their immersion in the realities of death, they acquire new visions of life and their viewpoints are broadened. They understand that they know something, but that this something is very little. Thus they dedicate themselves to important crusades and, within those, they help and learn. Workers from other circles of human experience find themselves in the same situation. They help and are helped. It could be no other way. We know that no miracles can violate the laws of nature. We are brothers and sisters to each other, evolving together, in a process of interdependence, which stresses individual effort."

This explanation satisfied us. Mrs. Ambrosina sat down next to the leader of the session, a man with grey hair and a pleasant countenance, who had organized the head table with fourteen people of simplicity and faith.

While Gabriel sat next to the medium, passing wide-reaching blessings on to her, as if to prepare her for the evening's activities, the leader of the meeting gave a sensitive prayer. After that, an edifying text was read from a book of doctrine, accompanied by a brief evangelical comment, the choice of which was influenced by Gabriel. Patience emerged as the overriding theme of the readings.

Really, the assembly as a whole seemed to be suffering from serious problems, demanding help to achieve balance once again. Dozens and dozens of people gathered behind the table, their tribulations and worries apparent on their faces .

Strange thought-forms arose from group to group, revealing their mental states. Here, darts of worry, knives of bitterness, clouds of tears... Over there, obsessive individuals wrapped in discouragement or desperation, and others exhibiting aggressive desire for revenge, worsened by fears of the unknown...

Discarnate souls in great numbers earnestly hoped for heaven, while others feared hell, confused by the false religious education they had received on the terrestrial plane. Several spiritual friends near the head table helped the leaders preach doctrine, lessons based on the evangelical theme of the night, spreading motivation and relief with their well-spoken comments.

Individual cases were not addressed by name, but we could clearly see that the sermons were delivered with an exact address. Here, a person heartbroken with discouragement was uplifted, there careless consciences were advised, and further on, forgiveness, faith, charity, hope were renewed...

There was no lack of persecuting spirits attempting to hypnotize their own victims, leading them into sleep so that they would not be aware of the transforming messages being sent to them. Many mediums were working in the room, collaborating to maintain order and harmony. Nonetheless, we saw that Mrs. Ambrosina was everyone's focus of trust and the object of their attention.

She was there as the heart of the sanctuary, giving and receiving, the live point of the silent junction between the inhabitants of the two different spheres.

Next to her, in prayer, a number of strips of paper were placed. There were requests, worries, and supplications from the people, seeking protection from beyond for life's afflictions and difficulties. Each paper carried an agonizing request, an emotional appeal.

Between Mrs. Ambrosina and Gabriel, an elastic shaft of bluish light extended, and spiritual friends, moved by Christian solidarity, entered the shaft, and one by one, took the medium's arm after influencing her cortical centers, attending to all the problems as far as possible.

However, before answering questions, a great fluid mirror was placed near the medium and, on its face, there quickly appeared the visage of each absent person who had been named in the evening's petitions. At a distance, the benefactors contemplated their images, gathered their thoughts, and detailed the persons' needs, offering possible solutions.

While knowledgeable companions of faith taught the path to interior peace, Mrs. Ambrosina, under the watch of instructors who prayed for assistance, was tirelessly psychographing.

The work in the room was now settling down and so we knew the time had come for our questions. Hilário was the first to speak, and he pointed to the enormous fluid band that linked Mrs. Ambrosina to the leader of the mission, and asked:

"What does that shaft mean, where the medium and the director are so intimately associated?"

Áulus, with his usual patience and benevolence, explained:

"The broadest development of mediunic faculties requires this measure. Listening and seeing, in the range of vibrations that transcend the common sensory field, Ambrosina cannot be at the mercy of all the requests from the spiritual sphere, at risk of losing her balance. When the medium is in the service of good, through good will, through study, and by understanding the responsibilities vested in her, she receives the closest support from experienced, wise spiritual friends who can guide her pilgrimage on earth by governing her powers. In the present case, Gabriel is the perfect controller of our friend's energies, so she only establishes contact with the spiritual plane under his supervision."

"You mean that in order to make communication through the intermediation of Mrs. Ambrosina, it will be necessary to tune in to her and to the leader at the same time?"

"Just so," responded Áulus, satisfied.

"A mediunic mandate requires order, security, and efficiency. The delegation of human authority involves granting resources from the person doing the delegating. Systematic cooperation cannot be asked of the medium without offering the necessary guarantees."

"Doesn't this make the process of exchange more difficult?"

"By no means. Before the respectable and understandable needs, with hope of real progress, Gabriel himself takes charge of everything to facilitate it, aiding in the communicators, just as he helps the medium."

Pointing out the perfect communion between the mentor and his pupil, I asked if an association of that degree was tied to commitments taken by the mediums before reincarnation, to which Áulus responded kindly:

"Oh, yes, such services do not take place without being planned. Happenstance is a word invented by men to cover up a lack of effort. Gabriel and Ambrosina planned this present experience, long before becoming involved in the heavy fluids of physical life."

"And why do you say," I continued, reminding the Assistant of his own words, " when the medium is focused on the service of good he receives support from a spiritual friend, if that spiritual friend and the medium have already been joined in brotherhood to each other for such a long time?"

The instructor looked at me and said:

"In any commitment, it would not be fair to diminish the value of freedom of action. Ambrosina became committed. That, however, did not prevent her from canceling the service contract, in spite of recognizing its excellence and magnitude. She could desire to find a new direction for her idealism, although she would be putting off deeds without which she will not rise freely in the world. The Spiritual Guides look for companions, not slaves. The medium who is worthy of being a helper is not an animal attached to a yoke, but rather a brother of humanity and an aspirer to wisdom. He must work and study for love... It is for this reason that many begin the journey but give up. Free to decide their own destiny, many times they prefer to do an internship with undesirable company, falling into fearful fascination. They start out enthusiastically in the work of good; however, in many circumstances they give ear to corrupting elements that visit them through their gaps of non-vigilance. And then, they trip and throw themselves into greed and laziness in personalized individuality that destroys, or in criminal sexuality, turning into toys of the adversaries of light, who suck out their strength, and annihilate their better potentiality. This is from an infinitude of experiences..."

"Yes, yes," I agreed, "but wouldn't it be possible for the spiritual mentors to take measures that would stop the abusers when they appear?"

My interlocutor smiled and spoke up:

"Each conscience marches by itself, in spite of there being many masters along the road. We owe victory or defeat to ourselves. Souls and collectivities acquire experiences with which they redeem themselves or rise up, at the cost of their own effort. Man constructs, destroys, and reconstructs destinies, as humanity makes and unmakes civilizations, seeking the best direction to answer the calls of God. That is why heavy tribulations wander through the world, such as infirmities, affliction, war, and decadence awakening souls to an ability to make fair discernment. Each one lies in the frame of his own conquests or his own debts. So, we see on the planet millions of creatures under the webs of tortuous mediumship, thousands holding substantial psychic potential; many try to develop their talents but rarely obtain a mediunic mandate for the work of brotherhood and of light. And, as we know, sublimated mediumship is a service that we should edify, even though this glorious process might take centuries."

"But, even in a mediunic mandate, can a worker in Mrs. Ambrosina's position fall?"

"Why not?" stressed the interlocutor. "A mandate is a delegation of power obtained through moral credit, without being an attempt at sanctification. With greater or lesser responsibilities, it is necessary to remember our obligations to Divine Law, in order to consolidate our titles of merit in eternal life."

And in a meaningful tone, he added:

"Let us remember the word of the Lord: 'much is asked of him who has been given much.'"

This conversation gave me a lot to think about. The valuable explanations of the Assistant, in reporting on mediumship, made me stay silent and reflective.

Such was not the case, however, with my companion, because Hilário, looked at the fluid mirror which functioned marvelously, and asked our guide for some explanation of it, for how it was able to show images of anguished people from moment to moment.

"It's a sort of television set, operated by sources from our sphere."

"Nevertheless," asked Hilário, seeking detail, "does

the face of the mirror display the vehicle of flesh or the soul itself?"

"The soul itself. By examining the perispirit, advice and conclusions are lined up. Many times it is necessary to analyze certain cases that are not presented; however, by gathering appeals in mass, we are able to organize ways to take care of them at a distance. For this reason, workers are distributed throughout different regions, where they capture images relating to the requests we get, tuning in to the emanations with our receiving capabilities. Television, which is beginning to spread around the world, may offer an analogy of such service, but our transmissions are much simpler, more precise, and instantaneous."

My colleague thought intently for a few moments, and said:

"What we see suggests some important ideas. Let us imagine that if someone were to issue a certain request to the mediunic mandate, subject to a certain delay between the request and the response... Let us suppose that the interested party, located far away, discerns what is happening and remains in spirit, as often happens, in a room at home or in some hospital bed, although already released from the physical body... In a case like that, will the response of the spiritual benefactors be delivered as if it were dedicated to the actual incarnate one?"

"This can happen under a variety of circumstances," added the Assistant, since we are not involved in automatic or miraculous service. We act in the spirit of cooperation and good will, depending on the success of cooperation, because a single part will not solve the problems of the whole machine. Workers who collect notes on the transmissions complain that they are too fast. Often, at a long distance, the suffering person is shown to those who would help her. The Samaritans of brotherhood with their obligation to help and by virtue of the large number of souls afflicted, cannot, on the spur of the moment, determine whether they are receiving reports about an incarnate or a discarnate soul, especially when they are not yet blessed with vast experience. In certain situations, the needy demand intensive help in a matter of minutes. Therefore, any mistake of this sort is perfectly understandable."

"But," replied Hilário, "wouldn't this disrupt the services? If it were us, the incarnate, would we not judge such events as being useless responses sent to dead people?"

"No, Hilário, we cannot view this in our terms. One who seeks faith earnestly will find the gift of clear and peaceful understanding, without being hampered by superficial and apparent contradictions."

At this point in the dialogue, the Assistant meditated for a moment and observed:

"But if the consultants are examples of light-mindedness and bad faith, approaching the mediunic work for the deliberate purpose of creating unbelief and dampening spiritual thirst, similar results, when verified, serve as just harvest of the thorns that they plant, since they abuse the generosity and patience of the friendly spirits and collect denial and mental torture for themselves. He who seeks a clean fountain, throwing mud in his face, cannot, thereafter, obtain pure water."

Hilário, now satisfied, went quiet.

And because two mediums of healing went to help the ill in a nearby room, while Mrs. Ambrosina and those who prayed were fulfilling their edifying duties, we sought the service of magnetic blessings, seeking new knowledge.

Xavier, Francisco Cândido. *Nos Domínios da Mediunidade.* **By the Spirit André Luiz. 32ⁿᵈ edition. Rio de Janeiro: FEB, 2005. [*In the Domains of Mediumship*]**

Chapter 15

Dom Pedro II's Chef

With his typical simplicity, Chico would tell us some quite surprising anecdotes that were normal for him.

When he was younger, Chico loved to cook. So, he liked to offer to cook a special meal for his good friend Jô (Joaquim Alves, 1911-1985), when he came to visit during his vacations. Jô was a book cover artist who did the covers of Chico's first two hundred books.

One day, while Jô was vacationing in Uberaba, Chico decided to cook, telling him: "Jô, at my side I have a spiritual friend, who brought along the recipe for a cake, which was the favorite cake of our remarkable Dom Pedro II [Emperor of Brazil from 1831 to 1889]. Actually, he's telling me that he was the Emperor's chef. Isn't that interesting?"

Interesting, yes, but the most interesting thing about these lessons is the friendships that are formed on both sides of life. And Chico had plenty of friends.

BIBLIOGRAPHICAL REFERENCES FOR RESEARCH

Friendship

A precious achievement friendship is the pollen of love, which prospers wherever flowers of feeling bloom in the generous tree of human dignity.

Franco, Divaldo P. *Sublime Expiação.* **By the Spirit Victor Hugo. 10th Ed. Rio de Janeiro: FEB, 2004.** [*Sublime Atonement*]

[...] friendship is a source of crystalline water, which rebuilds our strength in the long spiritual pilgrimage toward Jesus.

Xavier, Francisco Cândido. *Relicário de Luz.* **Several authors. 5th ed. Rio de Janeiro: FEB, 2005.** [*Reliquary of Light*]

Chapter 16

The Cat and the Bird

Early in the morning, Chico would have his breakfast, and with the leftover bread crumbs, he would feed the birds that came to his garden. The birds became used to the free food and came back regularly. One of them became particularly close, first posing on the window sill, and after some time, eating the bread crumbs from the medium's hand.

Chico had a lot of cats, and one of them would avidly watch the bird-feeding scene, day after day. The bird, now well fed, became fat and strong, and the cat paid him more and more attention. It didn't take long for his nature to take hold of him. On a Saturday morning, the bird was near Chico when the cat leapt up and caught the poor thing in its mouth.

Chico ran around after the cat but his attempts to save the poor creature were in vain. Nature won out.

The medium became sad and discouraged over the loss. He went into his room and when they called him for lunch, he said he wasn't hungry. When it was time for his afternoon snack, he again refused to eat. When they asked him if he was going to the Center, he said he might not because he was feeling so down. After great insistence, he finally agreed to have a bowl of chicken soup. When he finished it, Emmanuel appeared and asked:

"Can you tell me what's going on here?"

As if he didn't already know... Evolved spirits know what is happening with us, but they show us their humility even at these times, exhibiting ignorance so they don't hurt us in our most fragile moments.

"You don't know?" asked Chico.

"No! If I knew I wouldn't be asking you."

"One of my cats ate a poor little bird that used to come and eat from my hand every morning. This has made me sad."

"Interesting, Chico, what nature is like. I just saw someone eating chicken soup, even sucking on the bones without hesitation, but his cat couldn't eat a little bird? Get up, let's go to work."

BIBLIOGRAPHICAL REFERENCES FOR RESEARCH

To work

The worker for Jesus in this century will not only be his own conductor, but will also be a friend, a guide, a priest, and spiritual doctor to his suffering and needy brothers.

Xavier, Francisco Cândido. *Dicionário da Alma.* Several authors. Org. by Esmeraldo Campos Bittencourt. 5th ed. Rio de Janeiro: FEB, 2004. [*Dictionary of the Soul*]

When I refer to workers, I speak not of the companions who are completely well and have been redeemed, but of those who have the greatest superior qualities, on their way to full victory over the gross conditions and manifestations of life. In general, they are entities that are still in debt, but who have good will, perseverance, and sincerity that gives them the right to select the conditions of their reincarnation, thus deviating somewhat from the general pattern.

Xavier, Francisco Cândido. *Missionários da Luz.* By the Spirit André Luiz. 39th ed. Rio de Janeiro: FEB, 2004. Chapter 18. [*Missionaries of Light*]

The good worker is one who helps, maintaining

the necessary balance, doing all the beneficial work within his power, aware that his efforts express divine will.

Ibid.

Chapter 17

The Banana

Chico received a lot of visitors, both incarnate and discarnate. They were interesting, especially the naturalness of the visits.

One day, a spirit came to Chico, and as the medium tells it, he was wearing a very simple pair of overalls, like those worn by laborers. He sat next to the medium, who was near his kitchen table that had a bowl of oranges and bananas on it.

The spirit looked at the fruit bowl and asked:

"Mr. Chico, would you give me a banana to eat?"

Chico answered, "Take one. Feel at home."

The spirit took the banana, not in its material state, but rather a spiritual double of the fruit. He peeled and ate it. What impressed the medium was that the physical fruit turned black moments later, as if becoming extremely ripe.

The entity thanked Chico and Chico asked:

"What brings you around here?"

"Mr. Chico, I work nearby, at the city cemetery. My job is to help the newly dead."

"And what is your work like, my friend?"

"Many of the discarnate, Mr. Chico, don't understand the process of physical death; they become frightened and they don't want to leave their decaying body. Sometimes they are in such sad shape that I need to go into the tomb to pull them out and take them to receive the assistance they need on the spiritual plane. In many cases, the stench is unbearable, because of how long they have been dead."

Then Chico said: "Well, yes, sometimes we complain about our work, don't we?"

BIBLIOGRAPHICAL REFERENCES FOR RESEARCH
Astral Body –

"... all living beings ... from the most basic to the most complex, are dressed in an energy halo that corresponds to their nature. In man, however, this projection comes out profoundly enriched and modified by his thoughts and personality which cause the emanations of the cellular field to adjust to them, the known vital body or astral body...".

Xavier, Francisco Cândido. *Evolução em Dois Mundos*. By the Spirit André Luiz. 23ʳᵈ ed. Rio de Janeiro: FEB, 2005. (Pt. I, chapter 17). [*Evolution on Two Worlds*]

Disincarnation

... the union of the perispirit and carnal material, influenced by the life principle of the genetic germ, until this principle stops working because of the disorganization of the body. Maintained as an active force, the union is undone as soon as this force stops acting. Then, the perispirit becomes detached, molecule by molecule, and the spirit gets its freedom back. Thus, it is not the departure of the spirit that causes death of the body; rather death leads to departure of the spirit.

Kardec, Allan. *A Gênese: Os Milagres e as Predições Segundo o Espiritismo*. São Paulo: Edições FEESP, 2033 [sic] First Portuguese edition: FEB, 1944 [*Genesis: Miracles and Predictions According to Spiritism*]

... it is a moment of turmoil for the spirit that disincarnates. If the spirit is good, if it is pure, if it came to know the teachings of the Consoling Spirit in its physical life, it [death] will last but a short time and will not be painful. Up to a certain point, the spirit may, in this trance, be compared to a man who awakens, without clear awareness of his state, without knowing for sure if he is awake or still asleep. Soon, however, he gets ahold of himself and realizes exactly what his situation is. It is a moment of rapture, like that of a bird who escapes his little cage, and goes to join its companions in the air or in the branches.

Marchal, V. (Father). *O Espírito Consolador, ou Nossos Destinos.* 5th ed. Rio de Janeiro: FEB, 2005. [*The Comforting Spirit, or Our Destinies*]

Chapter 18

Two Hundred Years of Violence?

Nights spent in the company of Chico were always very special, and this one was no different.

We were with a friend, the speaker for the FEESP Spiritist Federation of the State of São Paulo, when he began a conversation with Chico about violence of our planetary society, saying:

"Chico, we are entering the decade of the 1990's, and we see violence increasing every day. How much longer is man going to live without respect for his neighbor, and not notice that this is against nature?"

The medium responded with great calm:

"Our Emmanuel tells us that if man wants it so, by using free agency, we will have another 200 years of violence in the world, only then to begin to live the Gospel of Jesus. "

It is important to emphasize in the teaching of Emmanuel through Chico: If man wants it so, in the use of his free agency... only then will we begin, look - will we begin - to live the Gospel of Jesus. It makes one think, and not only think, but want to work to reduce that length of time. After all, is it in our hands or not?

BIBLIOGRAPHICAL REFERENCES FOR RESEARCH

Violence

The word violence comes from the Latin word *violentia*, and it came in to use around 1215 to express the disrespectful use of force against the rights of a citizen. Almost three hundred years later, it came to mean any type of arbitrary abuse against another person, imposing one's will cruelly on another, and thus ignoring morality.

In modern days, violence has become a true epidemic, taking the form of control, aggressiveness, and rudeness, which causes all kinds of harm: psychological, moral, social, economic, and material harm, which almost always culminates in death... .

Violence is not inherent to the human condition, as a person is not naturally equipped with destructive tendencies to enjoy attacking and killing.

Violence, nonetheless, often occurs in maladjusted homes, resulting from indifference for one's partner, who becomes disposable when relationships are taken over by lasciviousness. Thus, changes occur in one's emotional behavior and the person may seek a variety of mates, in a sick thirst for new pleasures, which is always the result of psychological immaturity and spiritual primitivism.

Violence is also a destructive inheritance from the past, which still predominates in our animal nature, which breaks out, with or without justification, as if there were any justifications for returning to the barbarism from which humans should have already been freed.

This violence, which develops gradually, unhindered by unharmonious emotions, needs to be channeled toward love, while it is a curing force, like the water moving through a hydroelectric dam generating electricity.

Franco, Divaldo P. *Impermanência e Imortalidade.* **By the Spirit Carlos Torres Pastorino. 4**[th] **ed. Rio de Janeiro: FEB, 2005.** [*Impermanence and Immortality*]

The Spiritist Federation of the State of São Paulo (FEESP) is a non-profit civil, religious, philanthropic, and cultural society, whose goal is to teach, study, practice, and spread Spiritism in its three aspects: religious, philosophical, and scientific - in accordance with the work of Codification of Allan Kardec, and was founded on July 12, 1936.

Chapter 19

The Cart

Once when we were conversing with Chico in the wee hours of the morning, he told us of one of his experiences with Emmanuel, who was always giving the medium lessons.

Chico had pneumonia. He felt very bad, weakened by the disease, when Emmanuel appeared to him. Speaking to his mentor, Chico said:

"You know, I am feeling very bad, totally weak, as if it were very easy to leave my body. I think I am going to disincarnate."

Emmanuel was clear:

"You're not going to disincarnate."

"How can you be so sure?"

"You are not going to disincarnate and I can give

you a simple explanation. When you have a cart and you get a new donkey, you always have problems. The animal refuses to accept the bridle, it doesn't obey commands, you want to go to the right, he doesn't obey and goes to the left and so forth... When you have an old donkey, the situation is different. You put the animal in front of the cart and he knows exactly what he has to do. This is precisely your case, and that is why you are not going to disincarnate. Now do you understand?"

BIBLIOGRAPHICAL REFERENCES FOR RESEARCH

Disincarnation

For all of them [the spirits], disincarnation in obedience to the orders of the Greater Life means one more day of sanctifying work, so that they can once again head out on the road toward the dawn.

Xavier, Francisco Cândido. *Justiça Divina*. By the Spirit Emmanuel. 11th ed. Rio de Janeiro: FEB, 2006. [*Divine Justice*]

To disincarnate is to change from one plane to another, like someone moving from one city to another, there in the world, without it changing one's infirmities or virtues through a simple modification of the exterior.

Xavier, Francisco Cândido. *O Consolador.* **By the Spirit Emmanuel. 26**[th] **ed. Rio de Janeiro: FEB, 2006.** [*The Comforter*]

Chapter 20

The Machine

Once, while conversing with our group, Chico spoke to us about the importance of a typewriter (you, reader, depending on your age, may know of this machine from the Internet or as a museum piece), for doing the work with messages and texts received for publishable books.

Chico had a very old machine, with hard keys that required great effort to type his manuscripts. With Christmas coming soon, Mrs. Yolanda, president of our group, had the idea of buying a new typewriter as a present for the medium.

The workers of the Home Workshop got together and collected enough money to buy the gift: the latest model of a modern typewriter, which cost a fortune.

In order to get a more affordable price, the purchase was made directly at the factory. It was an electronic Facit, with the letters spread out in a circle on what was called a "daisy wheel." A beauty. A real tool for our days. A large part of the machine was made of metal and it came in a box protected completely by Styrofoam, cardboard, plastic... really something!

We took the typewriter to Uberaba. When we got to Chico's house, we left the machine hidden in the meeting room, so that after the psychographing and our conversation we could deliver the special gift. We could compare it today with all of the "iEverythings" that exist.

But every well-considered gift brings surprises, and ours was no exception. When we were close to taking our leave, one of the members of the group appeared with that enormous box and put it in front of Chico, to everyone's delight.

"Chico," said Mrs. Yolanda, "this is a present from all of us at the Home Workshop... ."

Chico was very pleased with the surprise and everyone was bubbling with gladness over his joy.

That was when one of the members of the group said: "Let's get the machine working... ."

Then we started a complex operation: open the box,

take out all of the packaging and protection, pull out the cable, and install everything, or almost everything. A big job. But when we plugged the machine in... NOTHING HAPPENED!

It wouldn't work at all. Our Apollo didn't work. What a disappointment! As always, at a time like that, we found an "expert," who believes he knows everything, but who doesn't know anything. We heard from the back of the room: "Leave it to me!"

Ready! Everyone thought it would be solved, and that we could leave knowing we had not given him a white elephant. Sweet illusion. After messing around with the typewriter, the only thing that our friend was able to do was get an interminable beep-beep, but no typing.

Chico watched everything calmly. We were all upset when the medium spoke with the tranquil attitude of a Mineiro:

"I think this machine is trying to tell us something!"

With his enormous love, he showed us how much we were stressed out, and worse, in the presence of a person who was an example of calm, tranquility and patience. The real annoyance was not with the machine, but our reaction to the problem. What a lesson!

The next morning, the machine was working perfectly, and was being used by Vivaldo, one of the people who helped Chico in transcribing messages and texts. The problem was a little plastic lock that held the daisy wheel, the part with the letters on it, but the real problem was our lack of vigilance...

BIBLIOGRAPHICAL REFERENCES FOR RESEARCH
Patience
True patience is always the manifestation of a soul that has achieved great love in himself and can give it to someone else by example.

Xavier, Francisco Cândido. *O Consolador.* **By the Spirit Emmanuel. 26th ed. Rio de Janeiro: FEB, 2006. [***The Comforter***]**

... patience is also a form of charity.

Xavier, Francisco Cândido. *Evangelho em Casa.* **By the Spirit Meimei. 12th ed. Rio de Janeiro: FEB, 2004. [***Gospel at Home***]**

Calm
... It is the substantial value for your difficult understandings.

Xavier, Francisco Cândido. *Agenda Cristã.* **By the Spirit André Luiz. 42nd ed. Rio de Janeiro: FEB, 2005. [***Christian Agenda***]**

Vigilance

The vigilance that Jesus counseled us to have has nothing to do with selfishness, cupidity, and the lower interests, or with terrestrial passions; rather it is joined to the pure, humble love from which it is born, to the sense of loyalty to goodness, to the higher purpose of maintaining faithfulness to justice and truth. It is the mail service between two worlds.

Sant'Anna, Hernani T. *Correio entre Dois Mundos.* **Diverse spirits. Rio de Janeiro: FEB, 1990.** [*Mail Between Two Worlds*]

Tolerance

Understanding and sympathy toward another person, whether regarding his opinions or behavior, or the right to believe what he wants, as he bases his attitudes that seem most compatible with his way of being, so long as they do not hurt other people's feelings, nor violate human dignity or society, constitutes tolerance.

... It is a measure of nobleness that reveals moral values and spiritual ascendency.

Franco, Divaldo P. *Estudos Espíritas.* **By the Spirit Joanna de Ângelis. 7th ed. Rio de Janeiro: FEB, 1999.** [*Spiritist Studies*]

Chapter 21

Little Message Boxes

One situation that impressed me tremendously were the famous little message boxes. It was hard not to be impressed by Chico's mediumship, attitudes, and the high level of vibration that surrounded him, a vibration we imagine is like that of Nosso Lar, 'our home.'

They were plain little boxes which carried messages to many people. Chico insisted on making them, putting the name and address of the recipient on them, and, as much as possible, taking them to the post office himself. Chico created hundreds of them and used them to answer the letters that came from all over Brazil and the world, asking for advice or prayers, etc. One day, we had not been visiting his home very long, when Chico asked me for my address. I wrote it down quickly without question, which was unusual for a young, curious person like me. A few days after our return to São Paulo, we were surprised to receive our first little box, one of so many that he would send us every month for years. It was interesting that the messages were always about something we were going through at the time, messages of motivation, comfort, perseverance, and so forth.

My curiosity grew each month. Once when we were at his house, I was able to see what happened with the famous little boxes. The letters piled up and Chico read the great majority of them; others he simply put his hands over, preparing the specific messages and then sending them. My curiosity exploded! I began to wonder what really happened in those cases. How could he know what type of message the people needed to receive? The answer was not long in coming. Using the faculty of psychometry, he could become aware of the content of the letters, and evaluate the needs of the senders.

In the same way, once a friend of Chico's, a member of a Spiritist Center in another state, took a present to Chico. It was a book, which was in a very well-wrapped package, and when the friend gave it to him, he said:

"Chico. When you get a chance, read this book and give me your opinion about it."

Chico picked up the package and without opening it, he said:

"Friend, this subject is very interesting," and he began to talk about the subject of the book, as if he had just finished reading it. He really had become aware of its contents through psychometry. When we left, the gentleman in question said to us:

"Surprising. However, I should be used to Chico; he is simply impossible! He didn't even open the package and made comments about the book's content that I hadn't even thought of. Incredible!"

A friend of ours, a Spiritist supporter, once said with propriety:

"Unfortunately, for a number of reasons, such as a lack of funds and prejudice, we have not studied Chico's mediumship very deeply. It is not only the mediunic question, but also we should have learned more about that missionary spirit who taught us so much."

BIBLIOGRAPHICAL REFERENCES FOR RESEARCH Psychometrist[4]

---

[4] The word psychometrist in English has two meanings: it can be the person who practices psychometry, or psychic perception by touching objects, as used here,

The psychometrist is, in sum, a type of seer, or rather an individual who has awakened the faculties and perceptions of the sort that the sleep walker only has when asleep.

Erny, Alfred. *O Psiquisimo Experimental: Estudo dos Fenômenos Psíquicos.* 3rd ed. Rio de Janeiro: FEB, 1982. [*Experimental Psychism; Study of Psychic Phenomena*]

Psychometry

... mediumship by which the sensitive person, put in contact with objects, people, or places related to past events, tunes in to the psychological climate of events, so that he or she becomes able to describe them with startling precision.

Anjos, Luciano dos; Miranda, Hermínio C. *Crônicas de Um e de Outro: de Kennedy ao Homem Artificial.* Rio de Janeiro: FEB, 1975. [*Chronicles of One and Another: From Kennedy to the Artificial Man*]

... the phenomena of psychometry... consist in putting an object in the hands of specially sensitive individuals, who can reveal the history of the object, or who will describe the person who used it long ago.

---

or it can be a professional who administers psychological tests, e. g. a member of the National Association of Psychometrists (http://napnet.org/). [Tr.'s note]

... possibility of establishing a psychic relationship with distant persons, unknown to all those present, but only under the condition of presenting to the sensitive person an object that the far-off individual has used for a long time and with whom one wants to communicate.

The modalities by which a connection is established between the sensitive person and the person or the surroundings concerning the psychometrized object; distinguish, in effect, psychometry from other forms of clairvoyance.

In psychometry... the objects presented to the sensitive individual... constitute truly competent intermediaries which, without favorable experimental conditions, serve to establish the relationship between the distant person or surroundings, on account of the real influence infused in the object by its possessor.

This influence, according to the psychometric hypothesis, would constitute such and such a property of inanimate matter to receive and retain, potentially, all types of physical vibrations and emanations, psychic and vital, just as happens with the cerebral substance, which has the property of receiving and latently sustaining the vibrations of thought.

... Ordinarily, the psychometric faculty is a function

of the subconscious integral EGO, since it is often verified with the intervention of discarnate entities.

Bozzano, Ernesto. *Os Enigmas da Psicometria: Dos Fenômenos de Telestesia.* Trans. by Manuel Quintão. 5th Ed. Rio de Janeiro: FEB, 1999. [*Enigmas of Psychometry: On Phenomena of Telesthesia*]

Umberto and Ms. Yolanda Cezar

Chapter 22

Spiritist Center in the Lower Zone

On a Wednesday, during an exciting conversation, Chico talked about some characteristics of the spiritual plane. He talked about Nosso Lar, which was undoubtedly one of the most stimulating topics. At a certain moment, someone asked:

"Chico, when you disincarnate, are you going to live in Nosso Lar?"

The medium responded: "Who, me? No way. If I could ask for anything, I would ask to set up a Spiritist center in the Lower Zone."

I couldn't resist and I said: "Thank God, Chico. Am I saved?" Certainly such a center will be a big success, since it will be well attended, and we will be able to ensure that we will literally go to HEAVEN - the CEU [a play on words: CEU is the acronym for 'Lower Zone Spiritist Center' - Centro Espírito do Umbral - in Portuguese, and also the word for 'heaven'].

BIBLIOGRAPHICAL REFERENCES FOR RESEARCH
Lower Zone

This region is populated also with discarnate beings and the millions of thought-forms bred by people everyday. Everyone radiates his or her particular thought patterns, no matter what plane they are on. Here is a fact for you to mull over: whatever else an individual is, he or she is also a nucleus that radiates forces - forces that can create, transform, or destroy. Science doesn't understand the mechanism yet, but there forces - in the form of ideas - are projected as waves. When we think, we create at some level. Thoughts are the way people on Earth communicate with individuals in the Lower Zone who have similar inclinations. Every soul is a powerful magnet...

Xavier, Francisco Cândido. *Nosso Lar - A Spiritual Home.* **By the Spirit André Luiz. Anon. English trans. Philadelphia: Allan Kardec Educational Society, 2000. P. 63**

Noting the fear that had overtaken me, Brother

Andrade explained to me in a low voice that the planes inhabited by the incarnate mind emitted troubled forms, if not horrifying ones, mixed with creations of inferior discarnate spirits. The majority of earthly creatures, in flesh or released from the body, make themselves known intimately through their almost irrational behavior. He stressed that the sphere next to common man, because of this, is populated by a real maelstrom of strange beings, capricious and often ferocious. He even said that innumerable wise men of superior spirituality classify such a region as an empire of the dragons of evil. I remembered the reading of certain mediunic pages before my death, and the dedicated companion confirmed my recollection, declaring that the zone in which we were traveling constituted an extremely vast threshold, between the residence of incarnate brethren and the neighboring circles.

Xavier, Francisco Cândido. *Voltei*. By the Spirit Brother Jacob. 24th ed. Rio de Janeiro: FEB, 2005. [*I Have Returned*]

Chapter 23

Full of Cats

On a Thursday, in the middle of summer in Uberaba, one more lesson awaited us on a visit by our Augusto Cezar Home Workshop Group to Chico's home. We got to his house around 7:30 pm. The day had been very hot and the evening continued to feel hot.

At that time, Chico had a number of cats, in addition to his dog named Brinquinho. When we got there, we went to the room at the back of the house and waited for the medium. That night, a lot of people had come to see Chico. We waited for him for a little over an hour. This was never a problem; on the contrary, the fact that we were in his home was reason enough for great joy.

As we entered the room, because of the stifling heat and the fact that the doors and windows were closed, we smelled cat urine. A friend would later confide: "Wow! What a smell of cat pee! It's very strong." And that's where it ended.

Some time later, Chico appeared and greeted all of us with that special Mineiro way of his, polite and calm. He wanted to talk with us, and was very happy for the visit. We all returned his greetings, when suddenly, Chico turned to the mentioned companion and said:

"You know, my friend. I love cats. That's why I have so many." Then he asked: "Do you like cats?"

"I love them, Chico," he answered, just a little worried.

"Really? And do you have one?"

And the friend, anticipating what was coming, said: "I don't, but I'm thinking about buying one."

"As I said, I love mine because they chase the rats that want to eat my books. Sometimes the smell of their urine stays in some places, isn't that right?"

"Yes, Chico. But I didn't notice any." The friend didn't know what else to say.

At a distance, Chico had read his thoughts about the strong smell of cat urine.

BIBLIOGRAPHICAL REFERENCES FOR RESEARCH
Spiritist book

... is a safe investment that improves our life, offering inspiration and clarification for our entire existence.

It is the best present for a family member that we want to recruit with knowledge of the spiritual forces that govern human destiny; it is the best comfort for affliction; the best remedy for the ill; the best charity for the mal-adjusted.

Given as a present, sold, won in a drawing, or lent, a Spiritist book should be part of our efforts toward guaranteeing legitimate and renewing Spiritism in building a better world.

Simonetti, Richard. *Para Viver a Grande Mensagem.* 5th ed. Rio de Janeiro: FEB, 1991. [*In Order to Live the Great Message*]

Chapter 24

Different Stories with the Same Ending

Around two o'clock in the morning, Chico began to tell us about some very strange events, different from each other, but with incredibly similar endings.

The first case was that of a woman with a congenital visual deficiency. She had always been a happy person, in spite of her difficulty with sight. Her husband, children, relatives, and friends always admired her radiant happiness. She was a person full of life and had an excellent aura. One of her relatives enrolled her in a cornea donation program, and after a certain amount of time she was called in. She did the necessary tests and the doctor verified that her blindness, although with her since birth, was correctable. So surgery was set up.

From a medical point of view, the surgery was a success, to everyone's joy. The woman in question had gained her sight in a short time, after the necessary procedures. The transplant occurred without incident. However, her life changed drastically.

The reader may say: "Of course it changed, that's obvious. A blind person who gains the ability to see enjoys a divine blessing!" That is something that we dare not challenge. But the situation took an opposite turn. Starting at the moment when the woman began to see, her life was transformed into one of profound sadness. She began to feel weak, showed intense depression, and was out of harmony with her family and friends, and suffered all of the effects that sadness produces. She seemed to have lost the joy of living.

One day, while with her family, she surprised everyone by saying:

"I want to go back to being blind!"

"What? What sort of craziness is this? You can't be serious..." To which she replied:

"I feel that I don't deserve this blessing in my life. I'm not in a position to receive this benefit. I don't understand why, but I feel that I am not supposed to see in this existence." And then she listed a number of other arguments. How difficult it is to understand what is going on in the hearts of our fellow beings! What sort of trial did that person ask for that made vision a source of sadness and suffering?

Sometimes we may say: "It's karma! It's atonement or punishment!" We label others' problems superficially, problems that only the other person knows, if he or she even knows them. In most cases, only God, in His infinite mercy, knows the truth.

Remember Jesus and the blind man on the road who was going from Jerusalem to Jericho (John 9:1-14):

"And as Jesus passed by, He saw a man which was blind from his birth.

"And His disciples asked him, saying, Master, who did sin, this man or his parents, that he was born blind?

"Jesus answered, Neither hath this man sinned, nor his parents: but that the works of God should be made manifest in him.

"I must work the works of him that sent me, while it is day: the night cometh, when no man can work.

"As long as I am in the world, I am the light of the world.

"When he had thus spoken, he spat on the ground, and made clay of the spittle, and he anointed the eyes of the

blind man with the clay.

"And said unto him, Go, wash in the pool of Siloam (which is by interpretation, Sent). He went his way therefore, and washed, and came seeing.

"The neighbors therefore, and they which before had seen him that he was blind, said, Is not this he that sat and begged?

"Some said, This is he: others said, He is like him: but he said, I am he.

"Therefore said they unto him, How were thine eyes opened?

"He answered and said, A man that is called Jesus made clay, and anointed mine eyes, and said unto me, Go to the pool of Siloam, and wash: and I went and washed, and I received sight.

"Then said they unto him, Where is he? He said, I know not.

"They brought the Pharisees him that aforetime was blind.

"And it was the Sabbath day when Jesus made the clay, and opened his eyes."

The lady in question reported: "I'm going to talk with the doctor who operated on me and ask him to remove the corneas and transfer them, if possible, to some other person who needs them." The situation was complicated, because the doctor, of course, refused her request, sending her to a psychologist and then to a psychiatrist, but without any change of her attitude. "I want to go back to being blind!" The doctor was ethically against the request, saying that this would be a direct affront to the professional oath he had taken.

Chico did not have all the information about the procedures used to perform the operation, whether documents were prepared, recorded, and authorized by the woman, her relatives, and witnesses. But no matter how absurd it seems, the corneas were removed!

At this point in the conversation, our curiosity was about to explode and I couldn't hold back my question:

"Chico, what happened to her?"

"Umberto," he answered, with that Mineiro manner of his, "she went back to being happy! She returned to her routine life, blind and happy, getting along once again with her family and friends."

Only God knows the meanderings of our hearts.

Another case that Chico told us, which was similar, was also about a woman from Uberaba, who had had a sore on her leg for many years. After many unsuccessful treatments, performed with the assistance of friends and donated funds - since the people involved were very poor - the lady was transferred to a specialist in São Paulo. Evidently, it was a long treatment, but satisfactory results began to appear, until she was finally cured and the sore closed with a scar.

A similar story: a happy person, who had good relations with family and friends, but after the good medical results, she became a very unhappy individual. Her statements were almost identical: "I feel that I don't deserve this cure; I see that I need to have this kind of problem; it is pure intuition that I got this illness in order to heal me."

Chico told us that the woman rubbed lemon on the site of the sore to make it open up again. She achieved what she wanted and became happy once again.

A friend said: "Yes, Umberto, just imagine... unbelievable!"

I asked Chico about it: "Weren't they just trying to get sympathy from their families?"

"Charity? You mean to get more attention or something of the sort? No. We know that she had always lived very well with her so-called difficulties, and we have a spirit needing to gain some correction or wisdom, a person who knows that their problems embody their road to redemption and evolution. Whatever it was, through self-awareness, we find answers to our trials or state of atonement. Nothing more, nothing less, just what is necessary."

BIBLIOGRAPHICAL REFERENCES FOR RESEARCH
Trial

Trial is an infallible remedy for our lack of experience. Providence works with us like a cautious mother toward her child. When we resist its calls, when we refuse to follow its advice, it allows us to suffer deceptions and reversals, knowing that adversity is the teacher of prudence.

Denis, Leon. *Depois da Morte: Exposição da Doutrina dos Espíritos.* **Trans. by João Lourenço de Souza. 25th ed. , Rio de Janeiro: FEB, 2005.** [*After Death: Exposition of the Doctrine of the Spirits*]

The spirit is on trial when, feeling the need to evolve, of becoming good, it asked for and obtained an incarnation of suffering, in order to achieve the goal in sight.

It is a being that recognized the need to progress, and to rise above human miseries.

It is a spirit that is on the path to perfection.

Do Ó, Fernando. *Almas que Voltam.* **12th ed. Rio de Janeiro: FEB, 2005.** [*Souls that Return*]

... it is a demonstrative resource of our faith.

Xavier, Francisco Cândido. *Ideias e Ilustrações.*

Diverse spirits. 5th ed. Rio de Janeiro: FEB, 1993. [*Ideas and Illustrations*]
Atonement
Until the final vestiges of need disappear, atonement consists in physical and moral suffering that is the consequence thereof, whether in the present life or in the spiritual life after death, or even in a new corporal existence.

Kardec, Allan. *O Céu e o Inferno ou a Justiça Divina Segundo o Espiritismo.* Trans. by Manuel Justiniano Quintão. 57th ed. Rio de Janeiro: FEB, 2005. [*Heaven and Hell or Divine Justice According to Spiritism*]
The atonement spoken of in Spiritist Doctrine is nothing more than the purifying purgatory of evil that infected the spirit. The spirit, through atonement, restores its own health and becomes free from the impurities that afflict it and delay happiness.

T. Santana, Hernani. *Universo e Vida.* By the Spirit Áureo. 6th ed. Rio de Janeiro: FEB, 2005. [*Universe and Life*]

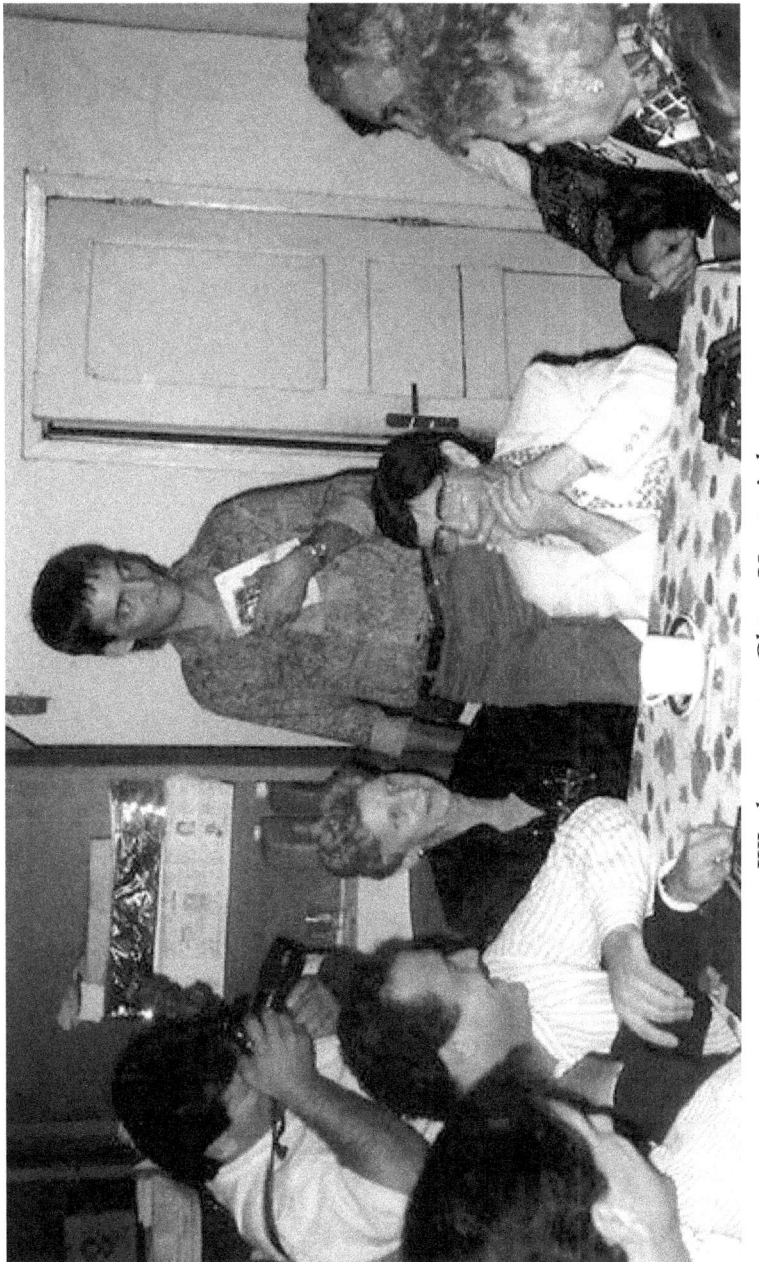

Work room in Chico Xavier's home

Chapter 25

ET's or Interpretations?

It was very common for people to make Interpretations and give opinions about the stories that Chico tells, along with their own experiences with the spirits; these people were not always very enlightened, as the great Codifier had alerted us in his writings:

"The spirits were no more than the souls of men who did not possess full wisdom nor complete science."

One time when we were with Chico, he told us of a visit he received when he had already retired to his room for the night: a spirit who was completely unknown to him came in, saying that he had a tale to tell. He said that he had witnessed the birth of Jesus, our Master. He began the story saying that Mary, the mother of Jesus, had a psychological pregnancy; and that on the night of the birth she had gone to sleep next to Joseph, her husband and the father of Jesus, when a spaceship arrived bringing the baby and depositing it at her side. The Three Kings, said the spirit, were really three extraterrestrial astronauts who had come to bring Jesus.

At the end of this story, the spirit asked Chico:

"Are you going to publish what I have just told you?"

And the medium answered very politely: "No, sir!"

And the Spirit then told him: "Do whatever you like with this information," and left.

Suddenly, Emmanuel, Chico's mentor, appeared, and Chico asked him: "Did you hear that story from the spirit that was just here?"

"Yes."

"And what did you think of my response?"

"You did very well."

The matter might have ended there, because regardless of whether from an incarnate or a discarnate spirit, we can make whatever interpretation that we wish to about any fact. To accept the idea that the Lord of the Earth, directly responsible for this planet, would need to set up a totally fantastic birth, not a natural one, is to want to imagine way too much. An undisputable reality is that while we have already imagined all sorts of possible situations about Chico, only a small minority actually do what he teaches.

Finally, that information about the birth of Jesus was passed on from one person to another as if Chico himself had endorsed it, with the usual statement: "Chico said it." Sometimes there have been additions like: "Chico said that that truth could be shared after his disincarnation..."

Well, my dear reader, isn't that a bit much? Fantasy has no limits, and because the discarnate is not here in our dimension to say that it is not true, should we believe everything we hear? As one character from a George Lucas film would say: "May the Force be with you!"

BIBLIOGRAPHICAL REFERENCES FOR RESEARCH
Kardec, Allan. *Obras Póstumas*. Trans. by Alceu Nunes. São Paulo: Edições FEESP, 2011. [*Posthumous Works*]

Mystification

To mystify, in its dictionary definition, is the act of deceiving, tricking, successfully abusing someone's credibility, to attract, using traps and subterfuge, malice, and even evil.

Pereira, Yvonne A. *Devassando o Invisível*. Under the direction of the medium's spirit-guides. 1st special ed. Rio de Janeiro: FEB, 2004. [*Revealing the Invisible*]

Mystifier

... there exist inoffensive mystifiers, just jokers, who pass time joyfully, if also frivolously, whose idleness and futilities only harm themselves.

Ibid.

Chapter 26

Son of Emmanuel

People were talking with Chico after his psychographing work at the meeting in his home for some mothers. There were messages of affection from their discarnate children, which not only comforted the hearts of those women, but also brought real lessons of love for all of us.

We began to ask about the third millennium, and also about the possibility that some spirit personalities would reincarnate during this thousand-year period. Chico always warned us of drastic changes, saying:

"People, the third millennium, as everybody knows, goes from 2000 to 3000. Changes will not occur overnight."

One of our colleagues then asked: "Chico, is Dr.

Bezerra de Menezes going to reincarnate in the third millennium?"

"I believe so," he answered. "Those spirits who stand out for good reincarnate to help our evolution." And the dialogue continued...

"So, Chico, will Emmanuel also reincarnate?"

"Yes, he will reincarnate."

"And will you come as his son?"

"Me? No!"

"Why not, Chico?"

"Why? Because Emmanuel is very demanding. I don't want to reincarnate as his son."

And we all laughed heartily with him.

BIBLIOGRAPHICAL REFERENCES FOR RESEARCH

Emmanuel

As was revealed in Two Thousand Years Ago... he was the Roman Senator Publius Cornelius Lentulus It can be deduced from the detailed description that he made of a dream that he was really Publius Lentulus Sura, then his great-grandfather, reincarnated.

... he left a famous letter, published in several languages, wherein he described Christ perfectly.

... he was a victim of the lava flow at Vesuvius; the spirit of Senator Publius Lentulus Cornelius disincarnated in Pompeii, in the year 79 A. D. , to be born after some time [approximately 10 years] in Judea where he would be the slave Nestorius, who continued his intense struggles for a long time in Ephesus. When he was an older man, he partook in the secret meetings with Christians in the catacombs of Rome.

The learned author of Two Thousand Years Ago, revealed that he was Father Manuel da Nóbrega, a famous Catholic priest in colonial Brazil.

... Father Nóbrega, along with Father Anchieta and other religious people, were the ones who implanted Christianity in Brazil ... he disincarnated on his birthday, October 18, 1570, at 53 years of age, having served for twenty-one consecutive years in Brazil.

Around 50 years later, he was reborn in Spain, where he was Father Damiano, vicar of the San Vicente church in Avila ...

These are the various reincarnations of the great Emmanuel, of whom we still hear news today... . the great friend of Brazil will return to the planetary struggle, "in the midst of incarnate Spiritists, at the end of this century [the twentieth], probably in the final decade."

Due to Emmanuel's clarity, sincerity, firmness,

and the loyalty with which he expresses his ideas, the teachings that he gives, and because of the most pure Christian morals that he demonstrates, has conquered unconditional confidence and respect of the vast legions of learners of the Good News of the Kingdom in Brazil.

Bérni, Duílio Lena. *Brasil, Mais Além!* 6th ed. Rio de Janeiro: FEB, 1999. [*Brazil, Further Beyond!*]
Dr. Bezerra de Menezes
... on August 29, 1831, this missionary was born in Riacho do Sangue, in the then Province of Ceará...

... The date of August 16, 1886 is memorable in Brazilian Spiritism because of what happened in the political, religious, and medical realms. One event had tumultuous repercussions, bringing great surprise and disappointment for many, primarily for professionals in the field of medicine. That was when Bezerra de Menezes, in one of the frequent Spiritist get-togethers that took place in the great Guarda Velha hall, in the presence of two thousand members of high society, solemnly proclaimed that he had joined Spiritism. His participation in the new religious movement was like a transfusion of new blood for the Doctrine in Brazil, which from then on took on a new, faster rate of growth.

Brito Soares, Sylvio. *Vida e Obra de Bezerra de*

Menezes. 11th ed. Rio de Janeiro: FEB, 2005. [*Life and Work of Bezerra de Menezes*]

Chapter 27

The Moon

We were conversing excitedly with Chico at his home when we discussed the great human achievements of the twentieth century. One of our friends mentioned the arrival of man on the moon, our natural satellite, which was visited for the first time on July 20, 1969.

Apollo 11 was the fifth manned mission in the Apollo Program and the first one to land on the moon. The crew consisted of astronauts Neil Armstrong, Edwin "Buzz" Aldrin, and Michael Collins. They fulfilled the goal proposed by President John F. Kennedy, when he declared before Congress in 1961: "I believe that this nation should commit itself to achieving the goal, before this decade is out, of landing a man on the moon and returning him safely to the earth."

Made up of the command module Columbia, the lunar Eagle and the service module, Apollo 11 with its three crewman aboard was launched from Cape Canaveral, Florida, on July 16, on the tip of a Saturn V rocket, in the view of thousands of spectators who filled roads, beaches and fields around the Kennedy Space Center and by millions of spectators on TV around the world, for the historic eight-day mission, which ended with a two-hour moon walk by Armstrong and Aldrin.

Chico told us: "It was really a great accomplishment. It's interesting that our Emmanuel told us that some of the astronauts would turn into mystics or become very religious after they visited the moon." As we know, there were several manned missions after the first one. I didn't wait a minute to shoot a question to Chico:

"Chico, did Emmanuel say there would be these changes in some of the astronauts?"

He told us that the moon acts like a satellite prison, reserved for spirits who have turned to evil. It serves for temporary isolation and treatment of the most recalcitrant among our brethren. Because the vibratory condition of these spirits is still not well materialized, because of their status of evolution, some astronauts felt moved, as if grabbed, giving the impression of hands and arms that were touching them or trying to hold on to them.

We were astonished at this story and even more aware that we really don't know anything.

BIBLIOGRAPHICAL REFERENCES FOR RESEARCH
The Guilty
... That is one who, by taking a detour, or by making a false movement of the soul, moves away from the objective of Creation, which consists in harmonious cultivation of the beautiful and the good idealized by the human archetype, by the Man-God, by Jesus Christ.

Kardec, Allan. *O Livro dos Espíritos*. Trans. by J. Herculano Pires. São Paulo: Edições FEESP, 1995. [*The Spirits' Book*]
Evil
Evil is any act practiced by the hands, by thought and by words that go against the Laws of God and which harms others and ourselves. The immediate consequences, or long-term ones, will always come to readjust, reeducate, and reconcile the indebted spirits, but all the work of Divine Justice comes in its own time.

Barcelos, Walter. *Sexo e Evolução*. 3rd ed. Rio de Janeiro: FEB, 2005. [*Sex and Evolution*]

... will always be represented by that sad inclination toward good only for ourselves, to be expressed in selfishness and vanity, in insensitivity and in pride, which indicates the permanence of the spirit in the lower lines.

Xavier, Francisco Cândido. *Ação e Reação*. **By the Spirit André Luiz. 26th ed. Rio de Janeiro: FEB, 2004.** [*Action and Reaction*]

... is always a closed circle around itself, temporarily guarding those that created it, as if it were a cist which dissolves, finally, into infinite good, as the intelligences that have attached themselves to him or take a liking to him become reeducated.

Xavier, Francisco Cândido. *Entre a Terra e o Céu*. **By the Spirit André Luiz. 23rd ed. Rio de Janeiro: FEB, 2005.** [*Between Earth and Heaven*]

Chapter 28

Message for Mothers

It was normal for the Augusto Cézar Home Workshop group, now led by Mrs. Yolanda Cezar, to include people who had recently lost family members. The great majority were usually mothers whose sons or daughters had returned to the spiritual plane while very young.

Chico attended to everyone with the simplicity and sympathy of one who knows the pain of a mother very well. In order to reduce the hurt in those hearts, the noble medium received messages from beloved family members, relieving the pain and suffering of those who sought him out, anxious for news of those who had departed.

For us, the messages served as great lessons of love

and affection, regardless of the dimension in which they lived.

We recall the message form a young man who had disincarnated at the age of seventeen. Through his mediumship, Chico described, in about 20 pages of material, what his life was like in spirituality.

He had disincarnated about two years before, and now he was coming back to tell some of the details about the place where he now lives. According to him, it was a duplication of the material plane, but of course in several ways improved.

The whole message was very interesting, mainly when it described things that had to do with his youth, since he had left at only seventeen. People would begin to fall in love and to court each other. Like all young men who are euphoric over a new love, he had sought out one of his mentors to talk about love, and was instructed as follows:

"Here on our plane feelings may be expressed in the most subtle way. For example, if we hold the hand of our beloved, we exchange higher and nobler energy from our feelings. There is no need for more expressive physical contact."

At this point, the boy said, through Chico's psychographing:

"Mother, in spite of the fact that our mentors still advise about this exchange of higher energies of feeling, I can tell you that it continues to be very difficult to only hold hands."

After finishing the reading, Chico told us:

"How immense is Divine goodness for us, right? On any plane of existence, we are cherished in accordance with our morals."

BIBLIOGRAPHICAL REFERENCES FOR RESEARCH
Relationships

Don't you remember Jesus's words in the Gospel: 'Love one another'? (John 13:34). When he said that, he wasn't just referring to charity in the strict sense of the word, because all of us have to learn, sooner or later, that giving - doing good - is simply our duty. No, he primarily wanted us to understand His words in the broader sense. That is to say, we are to sustain each other through mutual love and empathy. In the future, human beings will discover that tender words, mutual kindness and trust, understanding and friendly interest - all of which are the fruit of genuine love - are really the most stimulating food that life can take in. Naturally, when we're on Earth, obstructed by our physical natures, we operate under huge limitations that prevent us from seeing this clearly. But once we're back here, we know. We realize that lasting happiness and contentment are actually a matter of purely spiritual sustenance. Homes, villages, towns, and nations everywhere are built according to principles like this.

While she was talking, I found myself remembering different theories about the nature and meaning of love and sex that are widely held in the physical world. Laura seemed to guess these thoughts.

"No, Andy," she said, "you shouldn't think that it's all simply a matter of sex. Sex is a sacred expression of universal and Divine love. But it's only one of many expressions of that love's potential, which is infinite. Actually, more spiritualized couples find that tenderness, trust, mutual devotion, and understanding count for much more than physical relations. Sex very often becomes a transitory activity for them. In general, we can say that the exchanges of emotional intimacy establish necessary rhythms for the existence of harmony. For such couples the mere presence of the loved one, and sometimes simple understanding, is enough to nourish their joy."

At this point, Lisias other sister, Judith, took up the thread of the conversation.

"We learn here in Nosso Lar," she said, "that life

on Earth finds its point of equilibrium in love. But most incarnate people never realize the extent of truth in that statement. Twin, friendly, and empathetic souls form pairs and groups of every kind. They come together and help each other, and in this way sustain themselves in their projects of redemption. Take away that help, and a weaker person usually fails before completing the journey."

"As you see, Andy," Lisias added, "even here we're reminded of the lesson in the Gospel, 'One cannot live by bread alone." (Mat. 4:4)

Our talk was interrupted now by the ringing of the doorbell, Lisias got up to answer it, and a few seconds later, ushered in two polite young fellows, Polydor and Eustacius. They were, he said, friends from the Ministry of Education. We stood up and introduced ourselves; handshakes followed all around. After a few minutes, Laura said with a smile, "Well, I can imagine that you've all worked hard today, so don't change your plans on our account. I know very well that you're going to the Music Fields, and I suspect it's time you started out."

At these words Lisias's face wore the uneasy look of a conflicted man.

"Oh, go along, my love - don't keep Lavinia waiting,"

Laura said. "Our friend Andy will stay with me until he can go with you on your outings."

Xavier, Francisco Cândido. *Nosso Lar.* **By the Spirit André Luiz. Anonymous English translation by the Allan Kardec Education Society. Rio de Janeiro: FEB, 2000. Chapter 18. Pp 87-89.**

Chapter 29

Organ Donation

Chico regularly received messages for mothers looking for news of their little discarnate children. This happened both at meetings in his work space, a small room of his house, as well as at the meetings of the Prayer Spirit Group, where most of the messages were received.

For us, it was always a learning experience. We learned real lessons from the spirits who communicated to the hearts of family and friends.

Among so many messages received by Chico on Saturday nights, one stands out especially. It came from a young man who had died of an overdose of cocaine at the age of twenty-two. The message was extremely moving. At a certain point in the message, he really opened up to his mother, when he said:

"My dear mother, we both know that you shed many tears for me. At around sixteen, I entered the painful world of drugs, becoming substance-dependent. How sorry I am for the harm that I caused to myself, and mostly to your loving heart, as well as the pain and suffering that I brought to Father and other relatives and friends. Everyone fought to help me overcome my mortal dependence. Unfortunately, it was all in vain, since I succumbed to the intoxicating illusion of drugs. Some day I hope to be able to pay back everyone for the love that they poured out to me. I have been learning here in classes on the Gospel of Jesus that we are always free to sow what we wish, but the harvest is obligatory.

"To get the drugs that I could no longer live without, I began to commit little thefts, and then went on to armed muggings, putting my victims at grave risk for their lives, because I usually committed the crimes under the influence of cocaine, which destroyed my life quickly and brutally.

"The death of my body surprised me because I believed that that end was reserved for the weak, and not for me.

"My dear Mom, I ask you not to cry any more for me, and I want you to know that the last thing you did with my dead body was a source of great relief and help for me in our true homeland, which is the spiritual one. When you decided to donate my corneas so that someone else could have the blessing of sight, your gesture helped me tremendously to relieve the pain I was feeling, mainly moral pain.

"As I was told later, when I was finally able to realize the situation I was in, your charitable gesture removed me from blindness and ignorance about myself. Our friends on this spiritual plane told me:

"'Love from a mother's heart is a real blessing for us. In your case, your mother's attitude made it possible to reduce the pain and suffering that you inflicted upon yourself through your suicidal tendencies, leading to your premature death. This doesn't even include the responsibility I had for the harm I did to the people who were directly or indirectly injured by my thoughtlessness resulting from the drugs.

"Well, Mom, that's how it is. Today I am more aware of and responsible for my situation; I am in recovery from the dependency, and I ask you to bless me and wrap me in your love and affection.

"Your son forever..."

BIBLIOGRAPHICAL REFERENCES FOR RESEARCH
Organ Donation and Transplants

... At first, we thought that earthly medicine was a divine blessing, closely watched by spirits of great love and competence. Under the direction of Master Jesus, they took balsamic comforts to planet Earth at just the right time to treat diseases, providing a cure or relief from the pains of those ills.

Thus, the progress of medicine has protective spiritual approval. Of this there is no doubt.

Transplants provide a sublime comfort. They save lives. They relieve pain. They slide under the blade of a knife, since in the majority of cases they result from death (anticipated death for patients who otherwise would die within a short time; or death already occurred, in the case of voluntary or possibly involuntary donors.)

It is precisely for this reason that to Spiritists - who know very well what happens after death of the physical body - transplants bring about fear or actual terror. This should not be the case.

Organ Transplant and Codification

There is no specific mention of organ donation or transplant in the Codification of the Spiritist Doctrine. Nonetheless, without imposing a favorable understanding or appropriation of meaning, let us reflect on three questions commented on by evolved

Spirits recorded by Allan Kardec in the Spirit's Book. In isolation, they do not seem to favor any possible connection. However, these three cases, considered together, allow us to determine that there really is something there, although veiled. Let us see:

Question 156: "Are there cases in which blood is still in the veins, but there is no life?" This information, proclaimed in 1857, tells of a situation that perhaps we can consider as both encephalic death and brain death, diagnosed precisely only at the beginning of the twentieth century. In such a state, much more delicate than that of a coma, it may be supposed that the perispirit is already freed or in an advanced process of disconnection from the physical body; in either situation, physical pain will be absent from any somatic injury - extraction of an organ, for example - and the brain, by then irreparably "deactivated," no longer receives any message "of pain" issued by the central nervous system.

Question 257: "Theoretical Essay on Sensation in the Spirits: the perispirit only hears and feels what it wants" (here it appears that the teaching discloses that once disconnected from the physical body, the perispirit, which is the center of sensation, is able to select among them; organ donation is an act of love, understanding that the donor is already on the path toward disconnection with matter, and in this case, will not suffer any negative effects with the removal of some organ from his carnal dressing - already useless to him).

Comment: We still must consider the undeniable Father's Love toward all of His children; in the case of a recent death, the donor receives additional merit, a result of his letting go of material things (here the body that sheltered him and that will now inexorably decompose).

Question 723: "At the stage of humanity, flesh nourishes the flesh." Here we reflect that, if flesh nourishes flesh, there is nothing preventing us from applying the same idea to extract a lesson, but with a different focus: just as flesh nourishes flesh to sustain life, an organ (in good condition) replaces another (similar, but damaged), for a period of survival. It should also be considered that however long that period of survival (or improvement of life) goes on after a transplant, the person who received it will some day die, and then the Natural Law of Destruction - decomposition of the physical remains - will be fulfilled: the transplanted part will have the same destiny as the rest of the body, that is, it will return to nature.

We find in the Gospel According to Spiritism, Chapter I, item 3: "The body is nothing more than an accessory to it (the spirit), a covering, a piece of clothing (of the spirit), that he leaves when it is used up... On the occasion of death, he gets rid of it (the physical body)."

Adding another spiritual statement, we have Joanna de Ângelis philosophizing on the human body: "... A high divine loan, it is the instrument of spiritual evolution on the Earth... In the meantime, it also serves as a laboratory for experiments by which the Builders of Life, which, since millennia past, have been developing greater possibilities to culminate in an ever more perfected and healthy mechanism."

The word loan makes it clear that man, in truth, is not the owner of the body that he uses for his earthly pilgrimage, but rather, he is its user, or, if you prefer, its temporary occupant; serving as a laboratory for experimentation would seem to indicate that the altruism of organ donation for transplants among the living finds a basis.

Psychosomatic Rejection

We Spiritists know that every human being has a collection of positive and negative experiences accumulated throughout innumerable earthly existences, and therefore, comes the fact that no one is on exactly the same spiritual level. For this reason, because the donor's and receiver's perispiritual energetic vibrations are different, the transplanted organ will not find its vibrational frequency in the receiver's body. That is how organ rejection comes about, which mirrors differences in the complex and subtle vital systems of one and the other, regulating the balance between the planes - material and spiritual.

In this case, only with altruism on the part of the donor and gratitude from the recipient, we believe that this vibratory discrepancy will be diminished with the supervision of protecting spirits, thereby creating what the Spirit André Luiz calls "compensated vibrations." In transplants, we see an equalization of fluids, moving within the deepest layers of the psyche of the donor and the recipient.

Organ Donation: Material Disconnection

Taken together, the considerations presented above indicate that organ donation presupposes a disconnection from earthly goods - specifically the physical body - of which man is simply a user in passing. Thus, donating organs is an act of love, complementing those acts that were performed in life. It will only bring benefits to one who makes such a donation.

From the Divine Law of Action and Reaction, automatic and permanent action will greatly benefit the donor, in addition to the person benefitted (and his Guardian Angel), his relatives, friends, and the actual medical team involved; they will all be sending positive vibrations to the donor in prayers of gratitude. For a discarnate donor this is an incomparable blessing.

Considering that the physical body is included on the list of things that the Creator places at the disposal of a human being on his existential earthly journey, man should not consider himself the eternal owner of that material, but simply responsible for its good upkeep during the period of its use. Once that period is over, why worry about what destination it may take? If in this earthly phase there is an opportunity to make a final act of love toward one's neighbor, why not invest in that celestial savings account?

If a moral transformation can take place during the last minute of the life of one who is dying (see The Gospel According to Spiritism, Chapter 5, Item 28), consider that an organ recipient will have more than "one minute," rather a significant period of survival. No one continues to be the same after having had a transplant. Thus, self-reform.

NOTE: Obviously, not to donate organs is the right of each individual. And the non-donor can never be accused of selfishness or a lack of love for his neighbor. But, truth be told, one who donates demonstrates a praise-worthy position in terms of moral standing that can only generate spiritual benefits for him. The non-donor - and he alone - may answer this question for himself: "What if I need a transplant some day?"

Conclusion

We now turn the floor over to Dr. Raul Marino, Jr. neurosurgeon and Professor of Neurosurgery at the Neurosurgical Clinic at the Hospital das Clínicas of the University of São Paulo School of Medicine. We take his words as our own:

"... Heroes are hard to find: live donors, potential donors kept alive in ICUs, on artificial respirators and understanding families that have just suffered the tragedy of losing a loved one.

"It is necessary to have a high level of altruism, solidarity and generous Christian charity to transfer one's own life willingly after we leave our fleshly prisons, or allow a relative to share the gift of life with someone on the national list (of patients waiting to receive an organ), after a misfortune.

"... Transplants, intimately linked as they are to

the supreme act of making a donation, have appeared as if to test our virtues of human solidarity, our altruism, our generosity, our piety, our compassion, our philanthropy, our benevolence, our goodness, our love for our neighbor, our humanitarian spirit, our indulgence, our moral excellence, our greatness of soul, our mercy, our spirit of aid, support and help and, above all, the highest virtue declared in the Gospels: love and charity." (Folha de São Paulo, A3, "Opinião" May 15, 2001.)

Kühl, Eurípedes. *Revista Espiritismo & Ciência,* v. 4 [*Spiritism and Science Magazine*]

Chapter 30

The Heart in the Wallet

Chico's mediunic ability, his faithfulness to the content of the messages, his discipline, his humility and his profound respect for his spiritual friends and their messages were always impressive.

One night at a psychographing session at his home, Chico received a message that was more than twenty pages long from a young man who had disincarnated just over a year before. The letter was addressed to his mother, who was with the Workshop Home Group visiting Uberaba.

In this message, a curious fact caught Chico's attention. Near the end of the message, he began to draw and continued to do so for several minutes. It was not possible for us to see the drawing that the spirit was making through Chico's blessed hand due to the position he was in.

When the work was done, the received messages were read out. When the message with the drawing was announced, the young man's mother approached Chico for the reading. Several parts of the message touched everyone, but when Chico got to the last page, the mother's emotions were indescribable. Feeling very touched, she said: "Chico, that drawing at the end of the message is a blessing, an indisputable confirmation of the identity of my son."

The drawing was of a heart surrounded by flowers, and inside, the names of the young man and his mother.

The excited mother continued: "That same drawing was done by my son and given to me on the day of his disincarnation, just hours before the accident that ended his earthly existence. While saying goodbye to me, he said, 'Mom, look at this drawing I did for you.' And he handed me a little piece of paper with the same drawing that was reproduced at the end of the message."

Most impressive, the woman took a wallet from her purse, pulling a little piece of paper from it, with the drawing that her son had given her.

"Chico, I put this drawing in my wallet and not even my husband knew about it."

As she put her drawing next to the one drawn by the spirit through Chico's mediumship, it could be seen that they were identical, as if made by a copying machine.

When will we ever see anything like Chico's mediumship again?

BIBLIOGRAPHICAL REFERENCES FOR RESEARCH
Mechanical Mediumship

… The faculty of writing unconsciously on a wide variety of topics, science, philosophy, and literature, and using languages often unknown to the medium, has become known as mechanical mediumship. It is characterized by the absolute passivity of the medium during the communication. The spirit manifests itself indirectly in the hand, through the nerves in the hand; it gives an impulse that is completely independent of the medium's will, and the hand acts without interruption, so long as the spirit has something to say, and does not stop until it has finished.

The movements of the person who receives the message are purely automatic; we have seen mediums of this type hold a conversation while their hand was writing automatically.

... mechanical mediumship consists of writing communications, under the influence of the spirits, of which [the medium] is not aware, and of which he can only become aware once the spiritual influence has ceased.

Delanne, Gabriel. *O Espiritismo Perante a Ciência.* Trans. by Carlos Imbassahy. 4th ed. Rio de Janeiro: FEB, 2004. [*Spiritism Before Science*]

Chapter 31

The Room-Message for a Mother

Mrs. Yolanda Cezar, coordinator of the Home Workshop Group, would always invite women to come along on the visits to Uberaba. They were mothers who had lost a son or daughter and who were hoping for some relief for their grief through Chico's psychography.

The meetings took place at his home and he attended to everyone with sympathy and willingness. The messages, in spite of their personal nature, always revealed information about the condition of discarnate spirits and their lives in their spiritual homeland. A great amount of knowledge was gained from them.

Once, a member of our group made a very timely

observation. He said that at the meetings with Chico, we had the opportunity to experience a number of lessons from André Luiz, live and in color. That was an indisputable truth.

On one of these occasions, one of the women with our group received a message form her son who had disincarnated about a year before. He was sixteen years old, the victim of an accident. The message that Chico received was a long one. The young man shared a lot of information about his new home. He spoke of new friends and of relatives who had departed before him, and said that now they were working together.

But the most impressive thing was reserved for the end of the message. The boy mentioned his room, saying: "Mother, I know how much you love me and I want to say that I love you a lot too, and I respect you. But I have a favor to ask you, and I hope you understand. Please donate everything that I left on Earth to charity. I know of your affection for my things; however, leaving my room locked up and intact is painful for both you and me. I see your suffering and your pain whenever you go in there. Even the tennis racket that I left on my desk is in the same place. Please, don't turn my room into a temple of suffering. I am alive and well, and that is what matters most."

He ended with some words of affection for the whole family, expressing profound respect for his mother's pain.

It was inspiring for us to confirm the details with the mother, whom the medium had never met before. Chico's psychography was totally proven to accord with reality.

BIBLIOGRAPHICAL REFERENCES FOR RESEARCH
Psychography [also known as *automatic writing***]**
... transmission of thought from the spirit, through writing done by the hand of the medium. **Kardec, Allan.** *The Medium's Book.* São Paulo, Edições **FEESP, 2001.**
... It is psychic writing. The Spirit manifests itself by writing its message, and the manifestation is more nearly perfect as the medium's consciousness is less.

Imbassahy, Carlos. *O Espiritismo à Luz dos Fatos: Respostas às Objeções Formuladas à Parte Científica do Espiritismo.* 6th **ed. Rio de Janeiro: FEB, 2005.** [*Spiritism in the Light of the Facts: Answers to Objections Formulated Against the Scientific Part of Spiritism*]
... There are three different types of psychographic

mediumship: mechanical, intuitive, and semi-mechanical mediums.

With the mechanical medium, the spirit works directly on his hand, pushing it. What characterizes this type of mediumship is the absolute lack of awareness on the part of the medium of what his hand is writing. The movement of the hand is independent of the will of the writer; it moves without interruption, in spite of the medium, as long as the spirit has something to say, and stops only when the spirit has finished.

With the intuitive medium, transmission of thought serves as an intermediary between the spirit and the medium. The spirit, in this case, does not act on the hand to move it, but rather on the soul, identifying with it and imprinting its will and ideas. The soul receives the thought of the communicating spirit and transcribes it. In this situation, the medium writes voluntarily and is aware of what he is writing, although not writing down his own thoughts.

The semi-mechanical medium, or semi-intuitive, practices the other two types... The semi-mechanical medium feels a push in his hand coming from outside himself, but at the same time is aware of what he is writing as the words are formed.

Kardec, Allan. *Obras Póstumas.* **Trans. by Alceu**

Nunes. São Paulo: Edições FEESP. 2011. [*Posthumous Works*]

Resignation

... Conscious resignation is a mode of action. Man resigns himself in the face of that which is irremediable. Until he is sure that everything is over, he struggles in a healthy way for recovery of his lost sheep. Even in coming to terms with that which has no solution, his attitude should not be one of fruitless discouragement. Cultivating courage in the face of vicissitudes is in perfect harmony with Spiritist-Evangelical principles.

... True resignation is calm and conscious. The person assumes control of the situation in which he or she is involved, providing ways to reason and accept the consummate fact, so long as he actually does not have any way to undo it. Even so, resignation, and not discouragement, can be dressed in active character, reacting. How to react? By strengthening oneself in prayer and exemplifying the gospel lessons, for the purpose of overcoming the trial that has been imposed by Karmic law.

... Real resignation does not exclude the possibility of the person's reacting to overcome misfortune. Evidently, everything depends on the spiritual preparation of each person, and on the moral reserves that he possesses to protect him from the discouragement that precedes or follows despair, when the latter appears in such a way as to take form.

Mendes, Idalício. *Rumos Doutrinários*. 3rd ed. Rio de Janeiro: FEB, 2005. [*Doctrinary Pathways*]

Chapter 32

The Inebriated Driver

When one speaks of obsession or of some sort of spiritual influence, the subject always awakens curiosity. The case that we describe below is just one of so many early morning conversations we had at Chico's home. He was talking of the pernicious effects of alcohol in our lives, when he remembered a case whose protagonist was the father of a family and, of course, chemically dependent.

The man in question, as he left work, and before driving home, normally went to a bar near his home and would drink a large quantity of alcohol. When he got home, by now drunk, he would argue with his wife over anything and often would attack the poor lady.

The couple had one child, around twenty years old, who rarely witnessed this, since he worked during the day and studied at night. On one of these occasions, the boy was at home when the father arrived more drunk than usual. The argument with his wife started in front of the son and the situation became very complicated because at the height of the man's stupor, due to the drink, he went to get a gun he kept in his closet. He had had it for some time with the intention of killing her.

As the boy witnessed the scene, he tried to intervene, and in his attempts to hold his father's hands, trying to prevent the insane gesture, he accidentally caused the gun to shoot, mortally wounding the man.

After some time and amid much sadness, things began to clear up and life resumed its normal course. Unhappiness over the father's death would have to be overcome, because he had brought his disastrous end on to himself through his alcoholism.

My friend, you may be saying: "This type of case is not the first, nor the last." We agree in every way. Unfortunately, there will still be a lot of similar cases in the future. But the strange thing is that this was not the end of the story. Some situations surprise us with their unusual developments.

The discarnate man had a car. After his passing, the widow decided to get rid of the dead man's things, including his car. He had had great affection for the vehicle and kept it in the garage, driving it very little.

Some years later, their son had graduated and was working in a nearby city. He drove the distance every day in his car, leaving very early and returning in the evening. One day he was returning from work when a vehicle coming toward him crossed the road and collided head-on with his car. Both drivers died instantly.

After the investigation, it was shown that the driver responsible for the crash was inebriated. At this point, you may say: "This is very common on Brazilian roads. Unfortunately, there are still many who do not value their own lives, let alone those of other people."

The strangest thing about this situation is that the car of the drunk driver that caused the accident was the same one that had belonged to the dead father, sold some years before. Immediately, we asked Chico: "How did this happen?" To which Chico responded:

"Yes. The discarnate man was stuck to the car, as we see in André Luiz. Do you remember Os Mensageiros [The Messengers]?"

André told of a case when visiting Rio de Janeiro,

that while he was driving to Isabel's house, he noticed that many lower-order discarnate souls followed the pedestrians, or clung onto them. Many of the spirits were hanging out of vehicles, while others watched them from nearby windows. Some wandered through the streets in groups like dark clouds.

And he continued: "If love frees us, then hate holds us to situations and persons, isn't that right?"

"But Chico," I asked, "the son in question, isn't he a victim of circumstances? Of his father's free agency? Because he caused this whole tragedy with alcohol and his out-of-balance actions?"

"Yes, without doubt," answered Chico. "However, through our free agency, we can continue to carry on bad situations, right? How many times do we repeat the same mistakes, in spite of already knowing of our own weaknesses?"

"And as to the boy, wouldn't he be bringing more unresolved issues to a situation just as bad as the first?"

"How often do we make plans and yet still detour from our objectives?"

We again remember André Luiz in the work Os Mensageiros: "How many statements do we have from our brothers who planned victorious reincarnations for themselves, yet ended up very differently?"

At that moment we stopped asking questions, preferring to meditate on matters involving our own freedom of choice.

BIBLIOGRAPHICAL REFERENCES FOR RESEARCH
Free Agency
Free agency is defined as "the faculty that the individual has to determine his own conduct," or, in other words, the possibility that he has "two or more sufficient reasons to want or to act, to choose one of them and have it prevail over the others."

Calligaris, Rodolfo. *As Leis Morais: Segundo a Filosofia Espírita.* 12th ed. Rio de Janeiro: FEB, 2005. [*Moral Laws: According to Spiritist Philosophy*]

Free agency increases as the spirit advances, not just in knowledge, but primarily in morality. On the other hand, determinism is stronger when the spirit is more ignorant or crude.

There are spirits who give in to matter almost completely, or they live, we may say, in the service of matter itself: while there are others who, although subjected to physical organs, struggle constantly and are able to neutralize many of their needs through idealism, purity of thought, faith, and the burning desire to improve themselves. It's the contest between determinism and free agency. The more spiritualized side wins. The Spiritist Doctrine gives us another lesson regarding this: the body is not responsible for our mistakes, for our passions. No, it is only the instrument, since the thinking power is the spirit.

Amorim, Deolindo. *Análises Espíritas.* **Compilation by Celso Martins. 3rd ed. Rio de Janeiro: FEB, 2005.** [*Spiritist Analyses*]

Vice

The Spiritist Doctrine clarifies for us that all vices are harmful to psychosomatic forces, which destroy health and speed up death (and here we include alcoholism, gluttony, tobacco use, drugs, etc.) and they represent forms of indirect suicide, leading the spirit, post-mortem, to a feeling of guilt that is as great as the abuses committed.

Calligaris, Rodolfo. *Páginas de Espiritismo Cristão.* **4th ed. Rio de Janeiro: FEB, 1993.** [*Pages of Christian Spiritism*]

Alcohol

... Alcohol, which destroys thousands of creatures, is 'free poison, wherever it goes, and, in many cases, when one fantasizes about Champaign or whiskey, it becomes a guest of honor, consecrating social events. It flows down the throat of government ministers with the same lack of ceremony with which it rolls down the gullet of bums in the street. It drives famous artists mad, it pulls apart the character of selfless fathers, it brings about diseases, and it increases the numbers in insane asylums; cnevertheless, say this at a luxurious banquet and everything indicates that you, on the advice of your most generous friends, will be taken to a psychiatrist, if not right to a hospital.

Xavier, Francisco Cândido. *Cartas e Crônicas*. By the Spirit Brother X [Humberto de Campos]. 8th ed. , Rio de Janeiro: FEB, 1991. [*Letters and Chronicles*]

Alcoholic

Alcoholic... for the socio-moral consequences which it brings, when it becomes perverted into a criminal vice, simple at first and then abhorrent, it is the vehicle of cruel obsessors, opening up opportunities for discarnate alcoholics and impious vampirism, with consequent injuries to the physio-psychic mechanism.

Franco, Divaldo P. *Nos Bastidores da Obsessão*. By the Spirit Manoel P. de Miranda. 9th ed. Rio de Janeiro: FEB, 2003. [*In the Backstages of Obsession*]

An alcoholic is not only a destroyer of himself. He is a dangerous instrument of darkness, a live bridge for destructive forces of abysmal filth.

Xavier, Francisco Cândido. *Vozes do Grande Além.* **By various Spirits. 5thed. Rio de Janeiro: FEB, 2003.** [*Voices from the Great Beyond*]

Alcoholics and Drug Addicts

...they represent a group of psychopathic personalities, varying according to the degree of intoxication in which they are found and the injuries caused by abuse. More serious than physical injuries are those of a psychological nature, always present in so-called dependents.

Andréa, Jorge. *Visão Espírita nas Distonias Mentais.* **3rd ed. Rio de Janeiro: FEB , 1992.** [*Spiritist Vision of Mental Disturbances*]

Obsession

See "*Seven Obsessors for Each One*," **Chapter 37.**

Chapter 33

Paul and Steven

We were talking with Chico about the book *Paul and Steven*, when he began to tell of some curious events that occurred while he was psychographing that book. He said the work lasted three months.

His boss and friend on the Fazenda Modelo, Dr. Rômulo Joviano, gave him a little room so that Chico could psychograph the work in peace and quiet.

As soon as he began the work, Chico would have the company of a frog, which would come every day at the same time, at the exact moment in which he was starting to psychograph. Chico said: "He would come quietly, post himself in the corner of the room and stay there, quietly looking in my direction, and would not go away until the work of that day was done. That continued for three months. When Emmanuel put down the final period in the work, the frog disappeared and I never saw it again. Also, just imagine, looking at me for three months, there is no frog who would put up with it."

Then we asked the medium:

"Chico, what did you think was the most interesting thing about that work?"

"Emmanuel asked his spirit friends to place a device similar to screens around the space. I could see scenes taking place and I wrote them on paper. The scenes were presented like a live theater, as if I were inside them, without interference from me, of course. The realism was so great that it was possible to feel the characters' vibrations, and even sense the temperature of the places where the scenes had occurred.

"Emmanuel proceeded this way, because in spite of the fact that my psycography was mechanical, he didn't want me to imagine the scene, so there would be no type of interference on my part. Because the information was, after all, passing through my mediumship."

"Chico," we asked, "which of the scenes most caught your attention?"

"Undoubtedly, it was the moment when Paul, still

named Saul, fell from his mount and began to see Jesus."

We were all quite worked up at that moment. The medium did not tell us anything more, but it was probably that in the spiritual projections he was able to see Jesus, just as he presented himself to Paul.

BIBLIOGRAPHICAL REFERENCES FOR RESEARCH
Seer and Hearer Medium
Seers

Seer mediums are given the faculty to see spirits. Some enjoy this faculty while in a normal state, when they are completely awake, and they retain a precise memory of what they have seen. Others only have it when in a somnambulistic state, or near somnambulism... . The seer medium thinks he is seeing with his eyes, like those he really has with double vision; but, in reality, it is the soul that sees, and for this reason he can see both with the eyes closed and open, by which it may be concluded that a blind person can see spirits, in the same way that any other person can who has perfect vision.

Kardec, Allan. *O Livro dos Mediums* São Paulo: Edições FEESP, 2010. *[The Medium's Book]*.

Seer mediums: those who, in a state of vigilance, see spirits. Accidental and fortuitous seeing of a spirit, under special circumstances, is very frequent; but the habitual or voluntary seeing of spirits, without distinction, is exceptional.

Ibid.

Hearers

Hearer mediums hear spirits. Sometimes it is as if hearing an internal voice that resounds inside; other times it is an external voice, clear and distinct, just like a live person. Hearer mediums also can converse with the spirits. When they become used to conversing with certain spirits, they recognize them immediately by the sound of their voices.

Kardec, Allan. *Obras Póstumas*. Trans. Alceu Nunes. São Paulo: Edições FEESP, 2011. [*Posthumous Works*]

Auditory mediumship consists in the faculty to hear certain noises, certain words pronounced by spirits and that don't impress the ear under the usual conditions of life. It is necessary to distinguish two cases for this faculty: first, intuition; and second, real hearing.

Intuition occurs from soul to soul. It is a transmission of thoughts that works without the help of the senses, an interior voice that resounds inside the person; although the thoughts received are clear, they are not articulated with words and have nothing to do with matter.

In hearing, on the other hand, the words are pronounced in a way to be heard by the medium as if a person were standing there talking.

Delanne, Gabriel. *O Espiritismo Perante a Ciência.* **Trans. Carlos Imbassahy. 4**[th] **ed. Rio de Janeiro: FEB, 2004. [***Spiritism Before Science***]**

Chapter 34

The Uberaba Penitentiary

At the Prayer Spiritist Group in Uberaba there were always lines of people who wanted to say good-bye to Chico; in some cases, there were living lessons in those lines. On one of these occasions, Chico asked a certain couple who had participated in the meeting, as they were saying good-bye, "Listen, Mr. So-and-So, how's your daughter getting along?"

"Chico, right now she is hospitalized in a psychiatric clinic. She tried to commit suicide for the third time. Our grandchildren are with our son-in-law in his mother's house. It is a very delicate situation; the family is falling apart because of all the problems. We have tried a number of treatments and have had no results yet."

Chico, as could only be the case, gave them some

words of comfort, informing them that he would pray for everyone. However, before the couple left his presence, he said:

"Dr. Bezerra de Menezes (spirit) is here and he has a little suggestion for you. May I pass it on to you?"

"Of course, Chico."

"He suggests, if you accept it, that you begin doing charity work with the most needy people that you can find in Uberaba."

The couple, very emotional, gave their thanks and left.

Several months later, the couple returned to Chico's Center with news about their daughter: "Chico, we have come especially to thank you for having passed on Dr. Bezerra's suggestion."

"I'm not the person you should thank; I just work as a loudspeaker for the good spirits."

"Chico, however it is, we want to thank you and Dr. Bezerra. Our daughter is cured; she returned to her home and is happy at the side of her husband and children. We are all very happy and we want to share this joy with you."

The medium, happy and excited, thanked God, Jesus and His benefactor friends, but then he asked: "Please, tell me what happened."

"After you passed on Dr. Bezerra's suggestion to us, we went home to think about it. Who would the most needy people be? After some time, we came to the conclusion that some of the people being reeducated at the Uberaba Penitentiary had some of the greatest needs: abandonment and loneliness, they had no one, no family member or friend. We decided to visit them on Sundays. We began the visits some month ago and continued without interruption.

"So we took them blankets, books, cakes that we prepared at home, conversing with those brothers of ours, in routine visits, giving them our friendliness and company.

"As we visited our brothers, we began to perceive a considerable improvement in our daughter. She began to get balanced; her medication was reduced, until she was finally released. As you see, Chico, we are really happy."

The couple left happy.

After the couple had left, Chico asked Dr. Bezerra mentally what had happened in this case. Dr. Bezerra explained:

"When we made that unusual suggestion, they made the decision to begin working with our brothers at the Uberaba Penitentiary. On the spiritual plane, the discarnate mothers of those brothers of ours began to pay attention to that couple who was interested in their sons. After some time had passed, they decided to accompany them and they verified the situation of the couple's daughter. They noted that she was the target of a very intensive obsessive process. The mothers of those prisoners got together and decided that, as the couple was paying attention to their sons, they would pay attention to the daughter. And they began a job of explanation and evangelization with the obsessors, managing finally to get them to pardon her.

"Look, Chico, love is paid with love."

BIBLIOGRAPHICAL REFERENCES FOR RESEARCH

Obsession

From Latin *obsessione*. Impertinence, persecution, vexation. Concern over a particular idea that dominates the spirit in a sick way, the result or not of repressed ideas; fixed idea; mania.

Popularly, the word obsession is used to mean an idea fixed on a certain thing, generating a sick mental state, and possibly causing manias, tics, or strange attitudes.

Among us Spiritists, the term has a deeper meaning, as was spoken by the Codifier. Comparing the popular meaning of the word and Kardec's definition, we see that the "concern over a particular idea, that dominates the spirit in a sick way" can also result from guilt existing in the recesses of the mind, really denoting "persecution" to be transformed into the presence of an obsessor, who comes to avenge an old hangman or accomplice.

The master from Léon clarifies further: "... obsession always comes from moral imperfection, which gives ascendency to an evil spirit. It almost always expresses a vengeance taken by a spirit and whose origin is often found in the relationships that the obsessed one had with the obsessor in a prior existence."

... it is an obsession whenever someone, incarnate or discarnate, exercises a negative mental constriction over someone else - for whatever reason - through simple suggestion, induction, or coercion, for the purpose of domination; this process is repeated continuously on Earth or on the lower spiritual plane. Thus, we will have both the obsessor and the obsessed.

Shubert, Suely Caldas. *Obsessão/Desobsessão: Profilaxia e Terapêutica Espíritas.* **16th ed. Rio de Janeiro: FEB, 2004.** [*Obsession/Disobsession: Spiritist Prophylaxis and Therapy*]

Obsession. According to Allan Kardec, it is the

domination that some spirits achieve over certain persons. It is only practiced by inferior spirits, who attempt to dominate. Good spirits do not inflict constraint. They advise, they combat the influence of the evil and, if they are not heard, they retire. Bad spirits, on the other hand, attach themselves to those whom they can make their prisoners. If they do come to dominate someone, they identify themselves with the spirit of that person and lead it as if were a real child...

The causes of obsession vary, according to the character of the spirit. And, sometimes, they are taking vengeance on someone with whom they had some problem from another existence. Often, too ,there is nothing more than a desire to do evil: the spirit, because it is suffering, wants to make others suffer. It finds a sort of pleasure in tormenting them, in vexing them, and the impatience that the victim shows exacerbates the situation even more, because this is the goal of the spirit, while patience tires him out.

Obsession, in any modality, is a long-term illness, requiring specialized therapy of sure application and with results that are not felt quickly.

Treatment for obsession, as a result, is complicated, imposing a large dose of renunciation and abnegation on those who offer and administer such treatment. Mental transmission from mind to mind, obsession is an alarming syndrome that reveals a serious illness that is difficult to eradicate.

At first it is manifested as subtle inspiration, then worsens, so that with time the obsessive mind interferes with the incarnate mind which eventually reaches the climax of unfortunate possession.

It is a negative idea that becomes fixed, a mental field that weakens, giving desire to negative ideas that will come along.

In the same way, organic illnesses are manifest where there is need; the obsessive field relocates from the mind to the somatic arena, where moral imperfection of the past has left profound marks on the perispirit.

Franco, Divaldo P. *Nos Bastidores da Obsessão.* By the Spirit Manoel P. de Miranda. 9th ed. Rio de Janeiro: Feb, 2003. [*In the Backstages of Obsession*]

Chapter 35

Accompanying Chico

We used the title above to describe something extremely simple, that of being in the company of Chico in the room at the back of his house, where our meetings normally took place. That is also where we had our never-ending conversations in the early morning as we would walk with him to his bedroom. Just thirty feet, which usually took forty-five minutes or an hour to cover. That is because we often stopped while he told us one more "case" or gave us advice on some matter or other.

One night, most of the group from the Home Workshop had left with our leader, Mrs. Yolanda Cezar. As we said earlier, Chico always told Mrs.

Yolanda that he would stay on a bit to talk with the boys. A group of five or six young people would stay with him for a few more hours, until the medium would tell us that it was time for us to rest. Otherwise, no one would have left his presence. Our conversations lasted until three or four in the morning, and eventually we realized that Chico slept for a maximum of four hours per night, and we began to spare him to give him a chance for rest.

When Chico started to stand up, a little argument would ensue among those who wanted to support him as he walked to his bedroom. I generally lost no opportunity to offer, since I was always well positioned next to his chair, exactly on the side where he would get up - something of the "boy" in me with my twenty - some years. Surprises would follow, in the form of stories and rich comments because Chico knew that all of us were eager to learn more of Jesus, His Gospel, and the Spiritist Doctrine.

One thing that caught our attention was the natural floral perfume that Chico exhaled. When we held his hands, even after several hours of psychographing, his right hand sometimes was a little sweaty, and that was when the perfume was the strongest. To stand next to him, holding his arm, was to sense a perfume from

Heaven, if we can express it that way. At that moment, naturally we didn't want to make any comparison, or deifying, of Chico, but we imagined what Jesus might be like, his vibration, and the perfume that he naturally exhaled.

We know well that we are responsible for building ourselves up in the evolutionary process. It was exactly for that reason that we said above, that it was not a matter of deification, nor a privileged condition before Divine goodness, but rather an acquired achievement. God only knows how long a being takes to be able to exhale perfume through his vibration. In Chico's case, sometimes it was the smell of jasmine, other times of roses. Incredible!

We were able to be witness to many experiences of this, from people who would embrace him and leave with the perfume of a variety of flowers on their clothes, and in some of these cases, the clothing continued smelling of the medium's perfume for several days.

These smells invite studies and research within the Doctrine, and there is still a lot for us to learn. The Codification itself still brings us new revelations, as we continue studying and receiving teachings from the spirits.

BIBLIOGRAPHICAL REFERENCES FOR RESEARCH
Perfume

As we approached Chico, it was common for us to smell the perfumes that he radiated. These perfumes varied, and sometimes they were mixed with the strong smell of ether. We knew that they were produced by spirituality, which used his faculties.

The Apostle Paul, in a message in Chapter XV of The Gospel According to Spiritism, referring to those who practiced the maxim, "Without charity there is no salvation" affirms:

"Ye shall recognize them by the perfume of charity that they spread around themselves."

Chico Xavier was one of those.

When the perfumes did not materialize around the medium, the perfume of his aura remained, which was perceived by all of those possessing the greatest sensitivity.

We recall some of the events related to this faculty with our associates, among them, a woman from our community, who, while standing in line to take leave of the medium, saw another woman in front of her walk away with her handkerchief perfumed. When the woman's turn came, she placed a little handkerchief in her hand and, putting it in the medium's hand, asked him:

"Chico, give me a little of your perfume too."

Immediately, she felt her hand become moist and, when she pulled it back, the handkerchief was damp, exhaling soft perfume. Feeling great emotion, she kissed Chico's hand, and, as always, he repeated the gesture.

After showing the handkerchief to her friends, who confirmed the phenomenon, she put it away carefully and with affection. The little handkerchief retained the perfume for many days.

Grisi, Romeu and Sestini, Gerson. *Inesquecível Chico.* 1st ed. São Bernardo do Campo, SP: GEEM-Grupo Espírita Emmanuel, 2008. [*Unforgettable Chico*]

Chapter 36

Questions about Hitler and André Luiz

It was on rare occasions that we asked Chico about figures from recent history or Spiritist authors. One night, after the meeting at his home, while we were accompanying the medium to the door of his room we first asked about Hitler.

"Chico, Hitler, as we know, disincarnated in 1945, by suicide when Germany was about to surrender to the Allies. Where is he these days?"

Chico stopped walking, looked at us, thought for a moment, looked at us again, and answered:

"I understand your curiosity, but I can't say anything to you about it. If I did, Emmanuel would get me at night and give me a good beating."

We laughed a lot. However, we had no doubt that he knew the dictator's place on the spiritual plane.

On another occasion, also as we were leaving the meeting at his home, we asked about André Luiz. "Chico, who was André Luiz?"

And Chico told us the whole story.

"André Luiz was Carlos Chagas. I remember when Emmanuel came with him to our house to introduce him. We were in the little living room with one of our brothers, talking excitedly, when Emmanuel appeared in the company of the noble scientist, and said to us:

"Chico, this is our brother Carlos Chagas, who will also work with us, and will be responsible for various works, many of a scientific nature, beyond his personal experiences, and as soon as you are ready, you will be able to start the work."

Carlos Chagas thanked him and said:

"You know, Chico, I am still well known, as are members of my family. I think the best thing to do for the work is to use a pseudonym, to avoid any questions or problems."

And, turning to my brother, with whom we were conversing, he asked:

"What is the name of the boy who was sitting next to you?"

I answered: "It's my brother, André Luiz."

And the enlightened scientist then said to us:

"This is the pseudonym that I shall use, André Luiz."

BIBLIOGRAPHICAL REFERENCES FOR RESEARCH
Dr. Carlos Chagas
His Childhood

Carlos Ribeiro Justiniano das Chagas or, more simply, Carlos Chagas, was born on July 9, 1878, on the Bom Retiro Ranch in Oliveira, Minas Gerais. A descendent of a traditional Mineira family that produced coffee and cattle, he was raised there in a big colonial-style house, among the smells of tutu, tropeiro beans, corn bread, milk candy, fresh cheese, and guava paste... Oliveira was a small city with a strong tradition of citizenship. Public school instruction was quite advanced; there was a small but active press, represented by the Gazeta de Minas. Carlos Chagas' family was important in the cultural life of the city. Carlos, who had lost his father very young, greatly respected his uncles, but it was especially his mother, Mariana Cândida, a worthy woman with a great sense of the public good, who most influenced him. Even as an adult, Chagas would not smoke in her presence: it would show a lack of respect.

He began his studies at a Jesuit boarding school in the city of Itu in the state of São Paulo, and completed them in São João Del Rey, at the Colégio São Francisco, where he had an excellent professor, Father Sacramento. The priest would take his student into the field to observe and classify plants and animals, an activity that soon awakened the boy's interest in the natural sciences. Once his high school education was complete, his mother, with her unusual determination, decided that he should take a degree in mine engineering. In truth, Carlos Chagas wanted to be a doctor, like one of his uncles, but to satisfy Mariana Cândida, he gave in to her choice. He failed the entrance examinations. At the same time, he became ill; it appears that he was malnourished because of a deficient diet, so he returned home. One of his doctor uncles treated him, and their long conversations undoubtedly reinforced Carlos' desire to go into medicine. The uncle and his grandfather took charge of convincing his mother. Mariana had more faith in engineering - an objective "concrete" thing, she thought - than in taking care of sick people, but she finally agreed.

Carlos Chagas was accepted by the old Faculty of Medicine in Rio de Janeiro, which he began to attend in 1897. He didn't know Rio, but several of his friends, Mineiros like him, lived in the city. A cousin, Augusto das Chagas, was even a Federal Deputy.

He went to live in a boarding house for students in Tijuca, an aristocratic neighborhood, very lovely and full of trees. He then discovered that Tijuca was exceptional in this: in Catumbi, in Rio Comprido, in Lapa, houses were miserable, health conditions were horrendous, and diseases prevailed there. But, although it was a period of great political agitation, Carlos Chagas did not join any party, nor did he take on Positivist philosophy, like many of the young people of his time. Positivism, as we saw in the story of Oswaldo Cruz, was transformed in Brazil into a form of political action. Carlos Chagas was not interested. He intended to dedicate himself exclusively to medicine.

At the University

The study of medicine was a solemn matter. Students attended class in suits with vests, starched collars, and ties - which, in Rio de Janeiro's climate, was torture. The professors were even more formally dressed: they wore overcoats or grey morning coats, and top hats. That is to say: they imitated the Europeans, something that Oswaldo Cruz also did upon his return from Paris. The professors arrived at the faculty in elegant coaches (four-wheeled carriages with two seats, pulled by a pair of horses), they entered the auditorium, where the students were already seated, through a special door. Classes were lectures delivered in a doctoral tone. Many of the professors were famous: Chapôt-Prevost, professor of Histology (the science that studies tissues) and a well-known surgeon, who became famous for the very difficult operation of separating Siamese twins linked by the sternum (the bone in the center of the chest). Just as famous was Miguel Couto (1865-1934), a great clinician who later went into politics, of whom Chagas became a disciple; Couto showed him medical cases and advised him on his medical readings. One piece of advice was particularly useful: recommendations to study the work of Claude Bernard and Louis Pasteur. These two French scientists marked the history of medicine.

By the way, Chagas was a great reader. He devoured the works of José de Alencar, Bernardo Guimarães, Artur de Azevedo, Machado de Assis [major Brazilian authors of the 19th century], as well as Alexandre de Herculano, Eça de Queiroz, [leading Portuguese authors], and Anatole France. He even read in French, which he knew well, and which was the language of universal culture, the equivalent of English today. And this vast knowledge undoubtedly helped a great deal in his career. A good scientist is one who knows not only his own field, his specialty, but one who has a broad view of the world and society, something that great authors like Machado de Assis offered.

In addition to Miguel Couto, another physician also influenced the young Carlos Chagas: Francisco Fajardo, a specialist in malaria and a professor at the College. Fajardo took the initiative of giving a course on the disease. He needed an assistant, someone who knew how to prepare slides with patient blood, identifying the causative agent of malaria in the microscope. To his surprise, he discovered that Carlos Chagas, then in his fourth year of medicine, could fulfill such duties perfectly. In fact, Carlos was an exemplary student; not only did he do well in the laboratory, but he also followed the clinical subjects with great mastery. He worked with amazing dedication in the Santa Cruz clinics. He would do continuous turns, once spending a whole week there without going home, working with a colleague, also a relative, who had yellow fever and finally died of the disease. Among the students, he was known as "the student with two candles." At that time, study was done by candle light; in Carlos' case, having two candles meant a lot of study time. He only went out to visit the zoo.

However, a party changed his life. At the invitation of Miguel Couto, he attended a party at the home of a senator (from Minas Gerais, of course), Fernando Lobo. There he met Iris, the host's eldest daughter, with whom he fell in love. In a very uptight era like that one, it was not easy to court. But Carlos had the help of Fajardo, who brought him a note from the girl: she wanted to see him on Sunday on the streetcar that passed in front of the senator's house at four o'clock. And that's what Carlos did: he took the streetcar so Iris could see him, even from afar. This love affair at a distance lasted for some time, greatly hampered by the irregularity of the schedule of the vehicles, which were pulled by undependable mules or delayed because of rain. Also, Iris' mother was not in favor of the romance. Carlos was still a student, with no way to earn a living. In addition, the racist Maria Lobo suspected that he, in spite of being blond and having blue eyes, might have some Negro blood. Iris, distraught in love, locked herself in her room, and went on a hunger strike. Her parents finally consented to their courting, which resulted in marriage in 1904.

In 1902, about to graduate, Carlos Chagas met a doctor who would direct his career. At that time, to receive the diploma, it was necessary to write a doctoral thesis: a requirement later abandoned, notably because of the poor quality of the works submitted. At Francisco Fajardo's advice, he sought out Oswaldo Cruz at the Manguinhos Institute that he directed. Impressed with the young doctor's knowledge and seriousness, Oswaldo suggested he study malaria, which was then, as it still is today, a very common fatal disease. Carlos Chagas began to attend the Institute. Today the distance between the center of Rio and the Institute can be covered quickly by bus or car. At that time, however, the only transportation available was a boat that left from the Pharoux dock, (approximately where Praça XV is located, near the National History Museum) at seven in the morning, returning at six in the evening. And Oswaldo Cruz insisted that the schedule be rigorously adhered to.

Starting his Career

He defended his thesis in 1903, and immediately after that, Oswaldo Cruz invited him to work at the Institute. Carlos, in the meantime, had decided that his real vocation was to work with the sick. Thus, he asked to be transferred to the Jurujuba Hospital, which belonged to the government, where bubonic plague patients were treated - at the time a very common disease. He also opened an office in the center of Rio. He received patients sent by Miguel Couto and Salles Guerra, a friend of Oswaldo Cruz. He was a good doctor, but he didn't know how to charge patients; on the contrary, sometimes he gave money to them so they could buy the medications he prescribed. Thus, the clinic didn't cover its costs, especially since he was married and had a son.

That was when a new and decisive turn came to his life. The Santos Dock, in Itatinga on the São Paulo coast, was building a port, and the work had been stopped because malaria was attacking the workers. They asked Oswaldo Cruz to suggest a doctor who could help. Carlos Chagas, because of the subject of his thesis, was the perfect person for the job. By that time, the mode of transmission was well known, and Carlos Chagas' plan consisted primarily in combatting the mosquito that transmitted the disease. He had great success, and in three months the epidemic was mostly controlled.

Returning to Rio, Chagas was invited to work on the Manguinhos team, led by Oswaldo Cruz. With notable scientists - Rocha Lima, Arthur Neiva,

Beaurepaire Aragão, Ezequiel Dias - and with the regular participation of specially-invited European researchers, Manguinhos was the picture of scientific medicine in Brazil. Chagas especially collaborated with Max Hartmann, a renowned specialist in protozoans, a category that includes the plasmodia, the causative agent of malaria. He continued his field work in the fight against malaria in the Valley of Xerém, which supplied the water for Rio de Janeiro.

The Great Discovery

In 1909, Chagas was invited to another job, which would bring a great scientific opportunity to his life.

The Central Railroad of Brazil was carrying on a grand project: to unite by railway, the north and southeast of Brazil, from Belém do Pará to Rio de Janeiro. The work, however, was paralyzed - because of the usual malaria - at a village called Lassance, in the Mineiro brush land. Once again, Oswaldo Cruz was consulted and he again recommended Carlos Chagas, who left for that place in the company of Belisário Penna, taking laboratory equipment with him.

At Lassance, Chagas found many cases of a disease that had nothing to do with malaria. Many people complained of what they called *baticum*: palpitations, a sensation of the heart not beating normally. And it was not their imagination. There were many cases of cardiac insufficiency, that is, heart failure. And there were cases of sudden death for the same cause.

At that time, the diagnosis made in those cases was syphilis. It was a disease caused by a germ called *treponema*, which is transmitted through sexual contact. In advanced stages the disease attacks the cardio-vascular system. It was very common, mainly because there was no treatment - penicillin, which is very effective against treponema had not been discovered yet. The number of cases was very large; in Brazil the doctors said that "This syphilis is a necessary evil." In Lassance there was clearly a source of contagion: the prostitutes that flocked to the place to "service" the railroad workers. But the local residents, weakened by malaria, didn't seem particularly interested in sex. And, even among them, there were a large number of cases of this strange disease.

That fact caught Chagas' attention and demonstrated his real vocation : the true scientist does not let himself be led away by appearances, but rather goes beyond and tries to explore all aspects of a phenomenon, especially the most intriguing ones. This reminds us of a famous dialogue between Sherlock Holmes and his companion, Doctor

Watson. Sherlock Holmes is a character created by the Englishman Arthur Conan Doyle, who was both a writer and a physician, practicing medicine at a time when reasoning was highly valued in clinical practice. The doctor often acted like a detective, seeking the villain that caused diseases. In that dialogue, Holmes is talking with Watson about a crime and refers to the "curious incident" that happened at night with the watchdog of the house, where the crime occurred. "But the dog didn't do anything," protested Watson. "That is what is strange," replied Holmes. In fact, the dog should have barked at the approach of a stranger. Why didn't he?

This same curiosity struck Chagas. Common sense pointed toward syphilis, but if it weren't syphilis? What if it were some other disease? What could cause it? How would it be transmitted?

Chagas was in the midst of this quandary when a railroad engineer, Cantarino Motta, made a comment about the enormous number of barbeiros" in the place. Barbeiro is the name given to insects similar to the bedbug; they are nocturnal insects. During the day they hide in cracks in the adobe mud huts or in the walls of houses made of sticks. At night, they come out to bite the residents, on whose blood they feed themselves. Since people normally sleep under covers, they attack the face, and thus the name, which means 'barber. '

Examining the digestive tube of these insects under a microscope, Chagas made a great discovery: there was trypasonome, a single-celled parasite. In Africa, a variety of this parasite causes sleeping sickness, called that because of the sleepiness caused by the compromised central nervous system. At that time, the disease was in evidence: many regions of Africa were colonies of European countries, which sent their researchers there.

Now the disease in Lassance could be caused by a trypanosoma. Chagas decided to verify the hypothesis experimentally in monkeys, to see if the parasite could possibly infect mammals. But the marmoset monkeys of the most infected regions would not serve for the experiments. So he sent some barbeiros to Oswaldo Cruz, asking him to try to infect the monkeys in the laboratory, which Oswaldo Cruz did. Several anxious days passed, before the message came from Manguinhos that one of the monkeys had become ill. Chagas needed to go to Manguinhos to identify the trypanosoma. He left immediately.

"How much hope and how much anguish must have

assaulted his sprit during the long trip that he took?" asks Carlos Chagas Junior in the book that he wrote about his father. And it was, in fact, a long trip, with many detours and delays. He finally arrived. Oswaldo Cruz, as anxious as Chagas, sent an automobile to meet him at the train station, from which he went immediately to the Institute. There was the infected monkey, quite debilitated. The scientist took a sample of blood and examined it under the microscope: he found the same trypanosoma that he had seen in the barbeiros and monkeys of Lassance, later called Trypanosoma Cruzi, in honor of Oswaldo Cruz. The infection of mammals by T. Cruzi was proven. And how about infection of humans?

On February 14, 1909, a nine-month-old girl was brought to the pavilion that Chagas sometimes used to treat patients: there was no medical office there. The girl was Bernice, whom Chagas already knew and for whom he had great affection. The girl presented with a high fever and swelling on her face and body. She was not like the other sick people of Lassance; even so, Chagas decided to take the blood of the sick little girl. He examined it under the microscope and there he found Trypanosoma Cruzi. It was the first case in which he associated the parasite with the disease - and with this, Chagas had done something extraordinary, never done before in medicine: he had discovered a new disease, had identified its causative agent, and had found the mechanism of transmission.

Repercussions

The next step was to announce the discovery, which Chagas did in Brazilian and foreign journals. The National Academy of Medicine put together a commission of renowned doctors to go to Lassance to evaluate the work close at hand. After their audit was complete, they got together for a modest dinner under lamplight and that was where Miguel Couto proposed that the disease receive the name of Chagas, its discoverer. The proposal was accepted by all commission members.

Without delay, Chagas disease began to be identified in other countries of the Americas. Praises continued, culminating in 1912 with the Schaudinn Prize, a sort of Nobel of microbiology, the most famous names of the field participating in the selection.

Someone else might have sat basking in the glory. Not Chagas. He was a scientist, and science was the raison d'être of his life. That same year, he went to the Amazon accompanied by a team to do a survey of health problems in the region, a job started by

Oswaldo Cruz himself. The difficult mission lasted a year; he often slept in the open air in a hammock or on some improvised bed.

Returning to Rio, he was invited to go to Argentina, where his discovery was challenged by no less than Rudolph Kraus, head of the Bacteriology Institute of Buenos Aires. Kraus alleged that he had found barbeiros with trypanosoma in parts of Argentina without the parallel occurrence of cases of the disease. Chagas considered that perhaps the parasite had not yet adapted to human beings or - a more likely hypothesis - that doctors were not familiar with the diagnosis of the disease.

During his visit to Argentina, a picturesque incident occurred. Chagas went to visit Kraus' laboratory and left with an enormous overcoat which reached to his feet; it was Kraus' coat that he had taken by mistake. Chagas was the prototype of the distracted scientist the absent - minded professor - like those who become the butt of jokes. One time in his own house the maid served him a cup of coffee. He took money out of his pocket and laid it on the tray, "paying" for the coffee. Another time he received the visit of a young doctor who came with his wife to thank him for some favor. The visit went on longer than usual, and at a certain point, Chagas forgot that he was in his own home, and looked at his wife and said, "Iris, I think it's time to go home." But his distraction reached a high point when, at an international ceremony in Brussels, he received an important medal from King Albert of Belgium, but he forgot it and left it on the table. Later on, one of the King's orderlies took it to his hotel.

In this incident, he could have been the victim of his own subconscious, as Freud would say. After all, few things are worse than a boring visit, and maybe he really didn't give so much value to a royal medal (or did not value it so much as his own work).

Chagas, the Health Manager

When he returned from Argentina, he received some sad news: Oswaldo Cruz, who had been ill for some time, had gotten worse and had died on February 11, 1917. For Chagas, who had barely known his own father, Oswaldo Cruz had become more than a master, a true father figure for him. He was very taken aback. But, being the natural successor to the great health expert, that same month of February, he was named as director of the Institute. This required him to leave his laboratory research. From then on he would become, more than anything else, a manager. And a manager much sought after by the government.

The next year, an epidemic broke out in the country of the sadly famous Spanish flu (it is not known why it had that name, although it appears to have started in Spain, but that is not certain). From a Europe devastated by World War I, it spread throughout the world, carried by ship crews. In Rio de Janeiro, the disease immediately found many victims. In a thesis written the next year, the doctoral candidate Eduardo Imbassahy writes: "Almost the entire population fell to the terrible, fulminating breeze that came to us from western plagues; from one moment to the next, one of the happiest cities in the world became silent, a sad wasteland, with empty streets, closed houses, shuttered businesses, and unmoving vehicles." It was not even possible to bury the large number of the dead; prisoners were called on to do the service. There were not enough caskets, so the bodies were thrown into common graves, or picked up by private trucks that went through the streets, the drivers yelling "Any cadavers here?"

There was no vaccine against the disease, nor antibiotics to treat complications. All that could be done was to provide centers of care and hospital beds for the ill, a task that was assigned to Chagas by the President of the Republic, Venceslau Brás. It was essentially an administrative job, but a very difficult one: Chagas himself was sick and had to care for his family, his seriously ill wife and his two children. But he did the job so well that he was invited by political leaders to run for the Senate. He refused.

Still in this period he went about setting up a course in Tropical Medicine at the Medical Faculty of Rio de Janeiro. "Tropical Medicine" is an expression that is no longer used (in Manaus there is a Hospital of Tropical Medicine), but in the 19th century and beginning of the 20th, it enjoyed some prestige, more for political than geographical reasons: the "tropics" is where daring colonialist enterprises were carried out mining, exploitation of plant products, construction of railroads and other great works, such as the Panama Canal. So-called "tropical diseases" like yellow fever, malaria, the sleeping sickness, leishmaniasis, and others represented a big problem, both for the human lives that were snuffed out and for the economic losses that took place. With the end of colonial empires and with the realization that the microbes had no preference for the underdeveloped, a more scientifically accurate expression arose, "transmissible diseases."

The Glory and the Controversy

Chagas' prestige was enormous. He traveled

throughout the world, participating in conferences and scientific meetings. He received commendations and titles conferred by a number of governments, and was invited by the Committee on Hygiene (another term no longer used) of the League of Nations, the precursor of the United Nations, which has as one of its branches the World Health Organization. On these trips, he came to know world-renowned figures in medicine. In Toronto, he met the Canadian physicians and physiologists Frederick Banting (1891-1941) and Charles Best (1899-1978) who, some months before his visit, had discovered insulin: a revolution in the treatment of diabetes. A coincidence: a little later Chagas' wife was found to be diabetic and was successfully treated with Banting and Best's insulin.

In spite of this prestige, or perhaps because of it, Chagas found himself involved in controversies and unpleasant incidents. The first occurred at the National Academy of Medicine in 1922. Some members of the institution - which brought together famous doctors but had only a slight role on the scientific scene - put Chagas' work in doubt. The disease that carried his name perhaps did not exist or was a health problem restricted to the area around Lassance, affecting at the most, some dozens of persons. This argument was really a fight for power and prestige, but Chagas came out the winner, mostly because time proved that he was right.

Another incident occurred when he was returning from a trip to Europe in 1930. The ship had barely moored when an official came on board with an arrest warrant for him. That year, the famous revolution had occurred that swept Getúlio Vargas to power. As a Mineiro, Chagas had supported the Liberal Alliance, formed by politicians from his state and from São Paulo, which had opposed the movement. Meanwhile, the reason for his detention (which lasted only a few hours) was not exactly a political arrest, but rather, resulted from an accusation from a urologist who had a charlatan for a partner who claimed to be able to cure leprosy, a disease which had no effective treatment at that time. Chagas, as Director of Public Health, a position also held by Oswaldo Cruz, had ordered the doctor's office closed, and this was his first opportunity for revenge.

Chagas was criticized for a number of reasons, such as, for holding three different positions. Austregésilo de Athayde, later president of the Brazilian Academy of Letters, was a young journalist at the time who wrote: "Dr. Chagas wants to be on all the payrolls of the National Treasury: Director of the Manguinhos Institute, Director of the National Department of Public Health, Professor of Tropical Diseases at the Faculty of Medicine." That was true, although Chagas did not draw a salary as director of the Institute. In addition, until a short time ago, it was common for doctors to work in several places at once, even in public service. The Constitution allowed for it.

From the time of Oswaldo Cruz, Chagas also inherited controversy. One of them: the obligatory smallpox vaccine which he defended, as did his master. Smallpox was an epidemic disease from which the world was finally able to free itself at the end of the 1960's, thanks precisely to vaccination campaigns; at that time, however, there was a lot of discussion about it. Two arguments were used. In Germany where vaccination was obligatory, it was said that smallpox had caused 140,000 deaths, a half-truth: the vaccine was obligatory, yes, but only for military personnel, and the deaths were among civilians. When vaccination was spread to the entire population, the disease practically disappeared. The other argument was of a philosophical and political order: making vaccination obligatory violated individual freedom. But, observed Chagas, "those who advise the people to rebel against compulsory vaccination vaccinate themselves and their children." That is, 'do as I say, don't do as I do. ' Nonetheless, there was a certain authoritarian tone to these obligatory measures, and this was the cause of the dispute over the Health Code which Chagas, in line with Oswaldo, was proposing.

We must mention that during this time, the National Directorate of Public Health had been transformed in 1920 into the National Department of Public Health by decree of President Epitácio Pessoa. This change meant greater autonomy and better funding. As Director of the Department, Chagas took two types of measures. One was internal, creating Directorates that should cover various public health issues: oversight of foods, tuberculosis, leprosy, venereal diseases. These were vertical activities; from Rio de Janeiro, the agency in charge controlled actions executed throughout the country. The advantage of this is that action could be unified; the disadvantage was to lessen the power of states and cities, which saw themselves in the role of mere executors.

The other measure was the Health Code. With 1,194 articles, the Code regulated - from the point of view of public health - practically all human activities. It told people how to live, how to wash their clothes, how to build houses. Once again, from the technical and scientific point of view, the Code had a solid basis, but the way it was implemented generated protests, especially from the press, which attacked it almost with the same vehemence used against Oswaldo Cruz. One of the articles of the Code, for example, prohibited stables in residential areas. It was said that Chagas was acting in his own interest because he wanted to get rid of a stable located near his own home on Rua Paissandu. Indignant owners of stables almost invaded his residence.

Even worse problems came up as he was ending his term of management in 1926. The first of these was an outbreak of yellow fever, a result, according to Chagas' detractors, of a failure to fight the disease, which, however, had not been eradicated. Eradicating a disease means there are no more cases. That's different from control of a disease, in which public health is aware of cases and can prevent spread of the disease. Yellow fever came close to being controlled at some points, but it was never eradicated. Therefore, it could come back: as happened then and has happened recently.

The second problem was just as serious: an outbreak of smallpox occurred while Chagas was on a trip.

Upon his return, Chagas investigated the problem and found, to his surprise, that the vaccine had not worked because of technical defects in its preparation. He did not hesitate: he went to the press and told them what was happening. One more proof of his unassailable character.

He died relatively young, on November 8, 1934, at the age of 55, in the city of Rio de Janeiro, and had already become a legendary figure in medicine and science in Brazil.

A selection (with some small adaptations) from the book by Moacyr Scliar, *Oswaldo Cruz e Carlos Chagas: O Nascimento da Ciência no Brasil.* **Odysseus, 2007. [***Oswaldo Cruz and Carlos Chagas: the Birth of Science in Brazil***]**

Chapter 37

Seven Obsessors for Each

One thing about Chico's personality that impressed everyone was his good humor. He always had a funny story ready about others or himself, of converting some difficult situation into a source of joy. One of the best known of his stories concerns the airplane he was riding in, an event described on the Pinga Fogo program on the old TV Tupi network in July, 1971. This was one of Chico's favorite stories and one that he told several times during his life. Many writers and biographers of the medium have included this passage in their works, which is not only interesting, but very funny.

But if Chico used good humor to narrate events in his own life, other people did not always use good sense to interpret what Chico said. However, as they retold his stories they did not always do so with bad intentions.

One of the mistaken interpretations concerns obsessors. He was talking with a group of people when someone asked if all of us, reincarnated spirits here on Earth, would have the company of obsessors. The good-humored answer that Chico gave was: "The best will have SEVEN!" This phrase, meant to be funny, became absolute truth in many Spiritist centers, with the information that Chico had endorsed such an absurdity.

We are here playing the role of an advocate because we know our limitations and, if there is anyone who does not need any kind of defense, it is Chico Xavier, due to his exemplary life within the standards of the Gospel of Christ.

Without any particular basis, as we have said, the information about the seven obsessors spread, achieving the status of "doctrinal truth," when a simple mathematical calculation would serve to obliterate it. Let us see:

The population of the planet is estimated today at seven billion souls. If each person - the best people, naturally - had seven obsessors, that would mean forty-nine billion obsessors, just to make calculations easy. Using information from the Spirit Emmanuel, through Chico's psychography in the book Roteiro, [Route] (1952), Emmanuel states that the world-wide spiritual population of conscious discarnates was more than twenty billion spirits. At that time, the world incarnate population was around three billion. With this number, between the incarnate and discarnate, we have to become a gigantic importer of obsessors from other planets to be able to service the demand.

We recall a wise statement of a friend of ours during one of his brilliant talks, when he said good-humoredly: "If each one of the best people has seven obsessors, then as a Spiritist speaker I must have some twenty-one." He told us at the end of his talk that his Mentor, after he made that statement, told him, also with good humor: "You don't have that much going for you, to have twenty-one obsessors!"

BIBLIOGRAPHICAL REFERENCES FOR RESEARCH
Obsession
The Bezerra de Menezes Spiritist Group
What is Obsession?
Obsession is the domination that some spirits acquire over others, whether incarnate or discarnate, causing

them to psychic, emotional, and physical imbalances. It is a sort of moral constraint of an individual over another. It can be between an incarnate and another incarnate, and a discarnate over another discarnate. This negative, irrational influence brings people many problems, which make them ill in the soul, needing care, like any sick person. Normally treatment for obsession takes places in serious Kardecist Spiritist centers.

If obsession is a disease of the soul, what are its symptoms?

Obsession shows such symptoms as: anguish, depression, sleep problems (insomnia or nightmares), bad mood, lack of interest in study or work, social isolation, suicidal thoughts, lack of sexual control, etc. It is not to be concluded, however, that all people with these symptoms are obsessed. There are numerous other causes, known to medical science, which can cause similar symptoms.

And how can this spiritual disease be treated?

Obsession, as a disease of the soul, must be cured for good by an improvement of the individual in the moral and intellectual realms. Spiritism (Allan Kardec's doctrine) offers sure treatment for these diseases, since it treats the problem from the two sides of life. If it is caused by a discarnate spirit, the spirit will be called upon through specific evocations in serious meetings of spiritual interchange, in order to carry on a conversation to make the spirit aware of the evil that it is doing. On the incarnate side, treatment will be done through evangelization (moralization) and by fluid therapy (application of passes [blessings by the laying on of hands]), leading the person to an understanding of what he must do to free himself of evil.

How does a recently disincarnated spirit receive a new amorous affair had by his wife, still incarnate in the material world? Does he not accept it? Could he interfere in that relationship? Is there a waiting period for the incarnate spouse to have a new relationship without annoying the one who has died?

When the spirit separates from the flesh, the person goes into another dimension of life, which is spiritual. There he will have a new perception of things, having freer, fuller reasoning, since he is no longer confined to material limits. He understands that he will live new lessons, and the loved ones that he left on Earth will also have new experiences, necessary for individual and collective progress. Nonetheless, if he is a less advanced sprit, he may remain imprisoned in his mental world, reliving situations that he lived through in life, primarily if he cultivated passions and sentiments of exaggerated possession. Thus, he may suffer if his loved ones act with a seeming lack of affectionate interest in him, if they fight over inheritances or even if his "loves" become interested in other people. He may interfere in people's lives, often giving origin to obsessive processes. In such a case, spiritual help must be sought at a Kardecist Spiritist center, so that the problem can be faced properly. Of course, these situations are the exception. Normally, the one who has departed shows great understanding.

There is no specific time that is appropriate to have a new romantic involvement. That will depend on each person's situation. In true, sincere and long-lasting relationships, generally, when one departs and the other remains, a long time may pass before finding a replacement in his or her heart, if the person chooses not to remain alone. However, in difficult relationships, which are the overwhelming majority on the planet, the loss doesn't really become a problem. All of these things are governed by feelings. Time, in these cases, is of least importance.

I would like to know how to identify an obsession

of a discarnate by an incarnate soul. How can one become free of this?

We know that an obsession is a sort of constraint of one spirit over another, and that this occurs through the law of spiritual affinities. Therefore, bad influences can form from the incarnate to the discarnate. Generally this happens in a situation when there exists an unbalanced relationship between two individuals, both of "love" and of "hate." It may appear strange to say that love relationships may generate obsessive processes, but excessive and possessive love between two people (even between mother and son), produce the most diverse types of disequilibrium. If one of them disincarnates, the feeling remains the same, unless one of them becomes free through clarification. In the same way, cases of people who disincarnate leaving inheritances in which the heirs are dissatisfied, and who do not have good affectionate relations with the discarnate, can generate morbid fluidic conditions that involve the two planes of existence. The only way to become free of these problems is by seeking clarification, finding a Spiritist center that has experience in this type of help. Spiritual treatment, clarifying those involved in the process, together with a change in the attitude of the individual, is the key to spiritual problems of all types.

Can depression be related to obsession? How?

Moderate and serious obsessive processes almost always lead to a morbid mental state, which greatly favors depression, with all of the symptoms that the disease produces. In the meantime, not all depression can be attributed to spiritual influences. There exist organic mechanisms, resulting in failures of hormonal synthesis that explain depression scientifically. Evidently, even in those cases, there may be spiritual influences on the mental attitude of the person, although this may not be the causative agent of the process.

Is it possible for self-obsession to occur, that is, an incarnate person becomes obsessed with himself?

Yes, that possibility exists and is not rare. These are people who find themselves in a sickly mental condition, tormenting themselves. They live in a world of internal disharmony and they try to blame everything and everyone around them, generating greater and greater suffering for themselves and for the people they live with. The causes usually lie in the psychic problems of the individual, that is, in his own personal dramas. There are traumas, remorse, guilt, and situations coming from their intimate world and which harm their psychological stability.

Certainly, due to their mental attitude, they get in tune with a spiritual ambiance of the same kind, which aggravates the situation, although this may not be the determining cause of the disease. In addition to spiritual evangelization, they are normally helped tremendously by psychotherapy, through which they can be stimulated.

Could a convulsion be a symptom of obsession?

Generally, convulsions are not symptoms of obsession (although they may appear to be associated with the disease). Convulsions are actually caused by failures in the organic structure of the person, and need to be treated by specialized medical procedures. Changes in the senses caused by spiritual influences are not convulsions as defined by earthly medical science. However, care must be taken in dealing with people who have convulsive crises and who want to be treated in Spiritist centers. They may have epilepsy and need a medical evaluation. Crises of subjugation have some of the characteristics of epileptic seizures, but they are quite different. In epilepsy the person almost always loses consciousness and faints, with involuntary motor movements. In the crisis of subjugation, that is not the case. A sudden change in behavior may lead the perturbed person to fall to the ground; however he does not faint, but behaves as if he were a different person.

How should we proceed with a person who is under the influence of fascination?

Cases of fascination are very common among the incarnate, and they even occur within Spiritist center that deify their mediums or leaders. Before concluding that a person is a victim of a terrible fascination, it is necessary to use good sense. The problem should be taken for examination by specialized institutions that are not under the domination of our ideas, for their opinion. If we are certain of the obsession, we must attempt to guide the one who is suffering. After achieving the person's confidence, we must clarify the sick person little by little, letting him see the presence of the bad influence. What happens in the majority of cases is that he does not accept the idea of being affected by evil, the best thing to do in those cases is to leave the person in the hands of the influence that is affecting him. One can only learn through pain.

Credit: Spiritist website: www. espirito. org. br

Forgiveness

The concept of forgiveness, according to Spiritism, is identical to that in the Gospel, which is fundamental to it: an infinite granting of opportunities for the offender to repent, the sinner to recompose himself, and the criminal to free himself from evil and to rise up, redeemed for enlightened ascent.

He who forgives, according to the Spiritist-Christian concept, forgets about the offense. He does not hold resentment.

Help the offender, often without the person knowing about it.

Peralva, Martins. *Estudando o Evangelho.* **6ᵗʰ ed. Rio de Janeiro: FEB, 1992. [***Studying the Gospel***]**

Chapter 38

One of the Stories About Brinquinho the Dog

Brinquinho was one of many pets that Chico had during his life. He was a small dog. To someone who does not understand much about dog breeds, it can be said that he looked like a mixture of Pekingese and mongrel, or something like that. He was intelligent and playful. He loved to lick the faces of people when they held him on their lap.

One night, as we were driving to Chico's home, two women from the Home Workshop were talking excitedly and one of them said to the other: "You know, So-and-so, I love the visits that we make to Chico's house. They are always so reinvigorating, a marvelous environment, we feel like we are on a very high spiritual plane."

We always agree to that because the atmosphere around Chico was always full of light and surrounded by superior vibrations.

At this, the woman who was speaking added: "All of that, the teachings, work, messages and conversations with Chico are very gratifying, but that dog, that Brinquinho..."

"What an unpleasant dog, with that thing about licking our face... it's horrible."

The other friend answered: "So-and-so, don't say that! Just imagine if Chico read your thoughts!"

"Hogwash. He's not up to that."

And the matter went no further.

We had another meeting of learning and conversation, and Chico was happy to tell so many interesting "cases"...

In the early dawn, we lined up to say our goodbyes to our dear friend, but that night would not end without surprises. Anyway, with Chico it was common for us to have what we could call surprise lessons.

When the two women whose dialogue we quoted approached Chico, who came into the room? Brinquinho himself!

He immediately asked to climb into Chico's lap,

precisely at the moment at which the companion who had mentioned her dislike for the dog came up to Chico. Chico stopped for a second, and Brinquinho wagged his tail for our friend, when the medium said: "See, my friend, how Brinquinho likes you. He gets all excited in your presence. Isn't he cute?"

"Yes, Chico. That is true. He really is cute."

"So," said Chico, "put him in your lap. He'll like that a lot..."

Brinquinho did his usual thing: he pasted some loving licks on the woman's face.

You, my reader friend, may find it a coincidence. But such things do not exist in Universal Law. Did he or did he not read the person's thought? Did Chico attract the dog through his mental condition, to give the night's lesson? Or was it the Spirits?

That was not important at that moment, but rather the lesson. I never doubted that it was possible, because his ability to put animals at his side was impressive.

I remember that Chico held a Gospel in the Home meeting for his cats and dogs. He brought them together calmly around him to hear teachings from the Gospel. The main object was to calm Brinquinho down. I also recall Divaldo Pereira Franco saying in one of his talks, that the dog was so elevated that it must be the reincarnation of a dinosaur.

In summary: one who heard the story would be looking around and thinking: "My God, such simple, simple moments and passages, however always bringing lessons for us to reflect upon about our thoughts, our focus on material radiation, capable of being captured by better prepared and evolved minds."

BIBLIOGRAPHICAL REFERENCES FOR RESEARCH

Because it seems timely, we include here a small part of the information from the Spirit Bernard Pallissy, referring to the animals on the planet Jupiter and the evolution of those beings.

Familiar conversations from beyond the grave

Revista Espírita, April, 1858 [Spiritist Magazine]

Bernard Pallissy (March 9, 1858)

DESCRIPTION OF JUPITER

Note: We knew, from prior evocations, that Bernard Pallisy, the famous olive grower from the sixth century, inhabits Jupiter. The following replies confirm, in all points, that which was told to us about that planet at different periods, by other Spirits, and with the intermediation of different mediums. We think that they will be read with interest, as a complement to what we presented in our last issue. The similarity to the previous description that they present is a notable as, at least, an indication of accuracy.

The animals of Jupiter

48. Are the bodies of the animals there more material than those of men?

A. Yes: for them, the king is the terrestrial God.

49. Are there carnivorous animals among them?

A. The animals do not eat each other; they all live subject to man, loving each other.

50. But are there animals that are not subject to the actions of man, such as insects, fish, and birds?

A. No. All of them are useful to him.

51. We have been told that the animals are the servers and workers that execute material work, such as building houses, etc. Is this true?

A. Yes, man no longer lowers himself by serving other men.

52. Are the service animals linked to a person or to a family, or are they taken and traded at will, like here?

A. They are linked to a particular family; they can be exchanged as one pleases.

53. Are the service animals there in a state of slavery or freedom, are they property, or can they change their

master at will?

A. They are in a state of submission.

54. Do the worker animals receive any compensation for their efforts?

A. No.

55. Do the animals develop their faculties through some sort of education?

A. They do it by themselves.

56. Do the animals have a more precise and more characterized language than earthly animals?

A. Certainly.

Gospel at Home

The Spiritist Doctrine establishes the custom of studying and experiencing the message of Jesus within the home as basic therapy for recovery and sustenance of this divine institution. It is a resource that contributes to the balance of all members of the nuclear family, favoring renewal of their feelings, habits, and actions, and improving home life significantly. Gospel at Home is carried out using The Gospel According to Spiritism, since, in that book, the noble Spirits help us to understand the message of Jesus and put it into practice in our daily lives, based on the transcendence of life through the immortality of the spirit beyond this life.

It is not a formal religious service, uninteresting, and monotonous, but rather, is a rich experience of happiness and learning, in which everyone takes part, each one contributes a bit of himself: giving the opening prayer, doing the reading of the text from The Gospel According to Spiritism, guiding the simple comments about the text read, and dedicating himself to the vibrations, or giving the closing prayer. For this reason, it would be very useful to set a day and time apart when the whole family can be present, and keep the same time so that the Higher Spirits may reserve that time to be present among their many activities. Additionally, the commitment assumed to love reveals our interest in living it and keeping it as an extremely healthful habit in our lives. But let us not force anyone to accompany us, since if God respects our choices, what can we say about the freedom of our neighbor? God is a point of union, and never one of conflict or separation. May the most resistant be attracted as they observe the benefits that this time has generated in us, transforming us each day into better people in greater harmony with the Law of Love.

If there are children in our family, we should

motivate them to participate in this time of communion with Jesus. Our children, grandchildren, nephews, as well as all of us, are spirits from different places. They bring their successes, aspirations, and possibilities, but also urgent need to find themselves once again within the Divine Laws, and renew their feelings. It is fundamental to offer them the safe port of God, and a solid basis in the Gospel of Jesus, to offer them moral and ethical values that they will take from the home in building a more just and more brotherly society. In The Spirits' Book, question 582, Kardec advises us that fatherhood and motherhood are considered to be in the category of a "mission" or a "duty": "God places the child under the guardianship of its parents so that they may direct it to the pathway of good."

Certainly, once a week, we can all offer this time for the process of self-enlightenment, considering that it is not a matter of several hours, but of a relatively brief time, fifteen to thirty minutes. At these times, the noble spirits, messengers of Jesus, will approach the family, contributing with their inspiration, specific help, and exchange of energy, providing greater ease to better direct anyone who is ready to receive guidance.

Undoubtedly, it was Jesus himself, the Great Educator, who initiated this method, when in the home of Simon Peter, or in any other where he was a guest, or even on the lovely beaches of Capernaum, he brought his friends together and spoke with them of plans for constructing the Kingdom of God on Earth. On those occasions, comments would have been more profound and significant, because He would elucidate the group being prepared to carry out his work after his physical absence. Today comments on the text read should come from our deep and courageous reflections about our own behavior in life, toward our neighbor, and before God. It is critical that each participant utilize the text as a guide and model in order to renew his own behavior, picking up on other people's comments, and reflecting on what we can improve in ourselves within the lesson of the day. This habit serves as a link among all to learn to respect each other and to discuss common problems, without getting upset. This is a fundamental position to promote constructive dialogue and harmony, and the building peace within the home.

It is important for us to remember that it is not a mediumship meeting, so there is no need for any manifestation by the benefactors. It is a moment of learning, renewal, and connection with Jesus to carry out a reformulation of our values and ideals, and obtain spiritual support for these challenges.

It is a new habit that will facilitate development of appropriate behaviors. And evolution demands the institution of new habits, so that we can break away from inferior patterns in our march toward higher cycles of existence.

That which will build the world of Regeneration that we so much wish for will arise from within the home that has been saved and sustained by the Gospel of Jesus.

Spiritism proposes a new era, rich in brotherhood and solidarity, an era in which the experience of love will be the reflection of God, Our Father, in all people. The construction of this new world depends basically on strengthening family ties and salvage of the family.

In Jesus in the Home, Neio Lúcio recalls Jesus advising us: "The home crib is the first school and the first temple of the soul. The home of man is the legitimate exporter of characters for common life... If we do not become habituated to loving our nearest brother, in our everyday struggles, how can we respect our Eternal Father, who seems so distant?"

The Department of Gospel at Home has the goal of disseminating the Gospel of Jesus and the need to create and maintain a time in our homes for us to get to know and study the message of Jesus. This moment makes it possible:

GOALS:

- To understand the message of Jesus and to live it in our daily lives, identifying in Him the model and guide for our lives;
- To unite people, strengthen family ties and prepare to build a better world because of the moment of peace and understanding that Gospel in the Home offers;
- To make the book The Gospel According to Spiritism better known.

SCRIPT FOR HAVING THE GOSPEL AT HOME:

Choose a day and time during the week and invite the whole family. If they cannot attend or do not wish to, we will do it alone, only physically, in the certainty that Jesus will be present through His messengers.

START OF THE MEETING:

A simple, spontaneous prayer. We can also pray "The Lord's Prayer," as taught by Jesus, with pauses, paying attention to every phrase.

Reading from *THE GOSPEL ACCORDING TO SPIRITISM*:

Begin in Chapter I (skip the introduction) and

go to Chapter 28 on the Sunday Prayer ("The Lord's Prayer"), reading one item or a small section each week, always in sequence. If there are children or teenagers, invite them to participate.

COMMENTS ON THE TEXT READ:

Reflect on the reading, rereading the phrases that call the most attention. The comments should be short and simple, with the participation of everyone present. Avoid criticism of others' comments and try to apply the advice read for ONESELF.

VIBRATIONS:

TO VIBRATE is to emit and donate feelings and thoughts of love, tranquility, health, and peace.

TO VIBRATE is to love in thought!

TO VIBRATE for brotherhood, peace and balance of all humanity.

TO VIBRATE for the expansion and experience of the message of Jesus in all homes.

TO VIBRATE for our home, involving our family in love and harmony so that there will be union and peace among all.

HELP FOR CONCERNS OF THE MOMENT:

Ask for protection and support so that the moment's challenges, whether sentimental, material, physical, or spiritual, will involve this problem or this person in great light.

SECONDS OF SILENCE:

So that each person may talk with God, in the silence of his heart, not only of his needs, but also to thank God for all of the support that He gives us, and which we often fail to notice.

CLOSING PRAYER:

Simple and spontaneous. Here we can also pray the "The Lord's Prayer," as taught by Jesus, with pauses, paying attention to all of its phrases.

Anselmo, Maria de Cássia, and Others. *Estudo e Prática de Assistência Espiritual.* São Paulo: Edições FEESP, 2012. [*Study and Practice of Spiritual Assistance*]

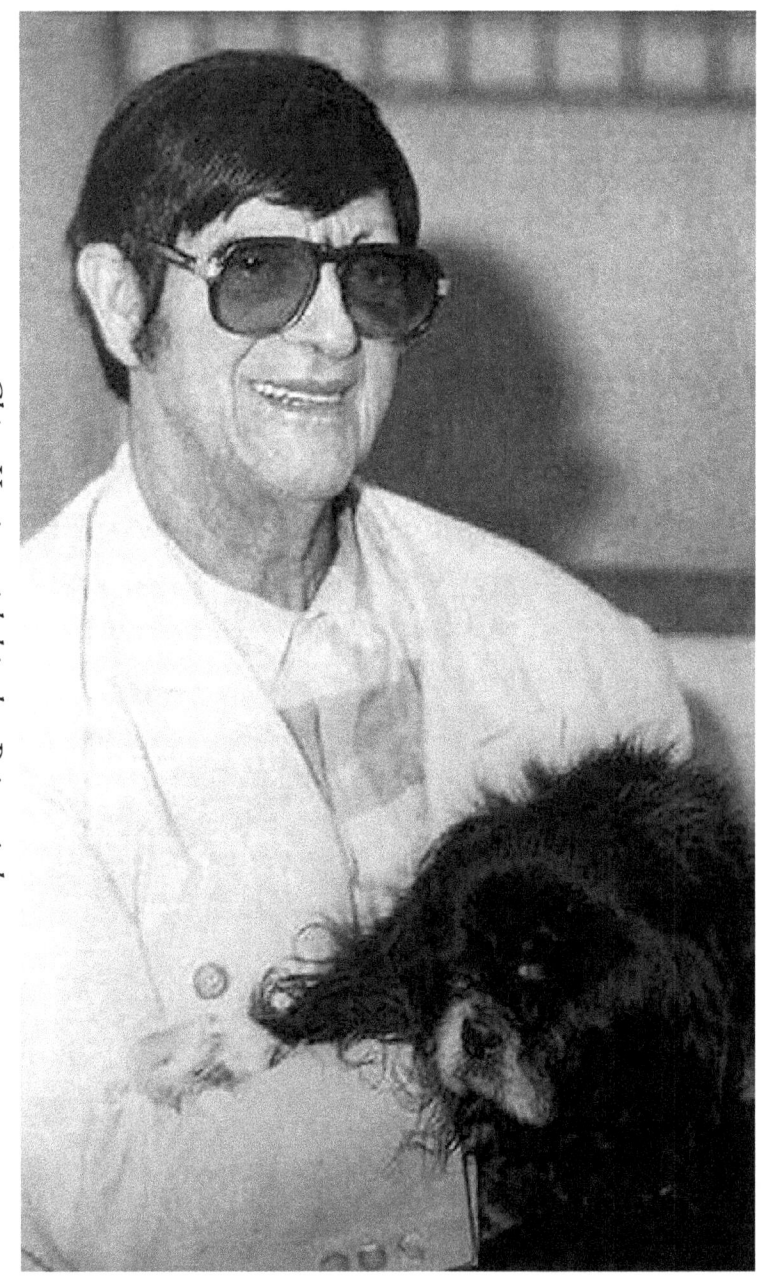
Chico Xavier with his dog Brinquinho

Chapter 39

Chico's Visits in Dreams

We were aware of the facility that Chico had to leave his body. However, there was probably much more to know than that which we were aware of.

On one of our visits to Uberaba, Chico was a little down about his health, and evidently none of us wanted to extend our visit to his home in order to allow his full recovery. We made quicker visits without getting into long conversations, which usually lasted for hours on end. One of our friends said: "It's too bad that Chico's health isn't great, because this time we can't talk with him as we have done before." We all agreed that the most important thing was his quick recovery, which always occurred because he had a great mission to carry out.

When Mrs. Yolanda went to visit him on Sunday, the day of our return to São Paulo, Chico said: "Yolanda, tell the boys," and that's what he lovingly called us, "that I'm going to visit them during the night for us to work and converse a bit."

We have always been faithful to Kardec's advice: it is necessary to pass everything through the screen of reason, study, and research, and not accept anything that violates good sense.

During the week after our return, on one of the nights, I had a dream about the medium, a real, live dream: we were working in attending to people, and the little bit that I remembered is that he was conversing with a group, and then we took our leave as always. I gave him a kiss on the cheek, which was immediately returned.

The next day, one of our friends who had been with us in Uberaba told me: "Interesting. Last night I dreamt about Chico." It could be interesting, but this was the time to compare, to check.

"And what was it like?" I asked.

To my surprise, his details were amazingly similar, with richness of detail. It was literally the confirmation of what he had said to D. Yolanda: "Tell the boys that I will visit them during the night for us to work and converse a bit."

BIBLIOGRAPHICAL REFERENCES FOR RESEARCH
Leaving the Body and Bilocation
Also see Chapter 3.
... it is at the same time fluidic, sensorial and psychic (bilocation), relocating the conscious personality of the sensitive individual to the fluidic body, who then perceives, at a distance, his own somatic body, inanimate and lifeless.

Bozzano, Ernesto. *Metapsíquica Humana.* Trans. by Araújo Franco. 5th ed. Rio de Janeiro: FEB, 2005. [*Human Metapsychic*]

Bilocation
With the generic denomination of "bilocation phenomenon" we designate the multiple modalities under which there occurs the mysterious fluidic departing of the bodily organism from the body. From these come the phenomena that are fundamentally important for the metapsychic disciplines, because they reveal the manifestations of the soul. These are inherent to the functions of the physical-psychic organism of a live being, and have as their center a certain substance that is qualitatively separate from the organism itself. For this reason, they take on a resolute theoretical value for the experimental demonstration

of the existence and survival of the human spirit.

In other words: the phenomena of bilocation demonstrate that in the somatic body there exists an ethereal body which, under rare circumstances of vital reduction in individuals (physiological, hypnotic or mediunic sleep, ecstasy, fainting, narcosis, or coma), is capable of temporarily leaving the somatic body during incarnate existence... the ethereal body is capable of being separated temporarily from the somatic body, with essential conservation of consciousness of itself...

Bozzano, Ernesto. *Animismo ou Espiritismo: Qual dos Dois Explica o Conjunto de Fatos?* **Trans. by Guillon Ribeiro. 5th ed. Rio de Janeiro: FEB, 1995.** [*Animism or Spiritism: Which of the Two Explains the Set of Facts?*]

Spiritist Dreams

In Spiritist dreams the soul, separated from the body, carries out real and loving work, finding ways for us to find ourselves with relatives, friends, and instructors, and also with our enemies both from this and from other lives.

Peralva, Martins. *Estudando a Mediunidade.* **23rd ed. Rio de Janeiro: FEB, 1996.** [*Studying Mediumship*]

"Dreams are the remembrance of what your spirit

has seen during sleep; but you must remark that you do not always dream, because you do not always remember what you have seen, or all that you have seen. Your dreams do not always reflect the action of your soul in its full development; for they are often only the reflex of the confusion that accompanies your departure or your return, mingled with the vague remembrance of what you have done, or of what has occupied your thoughts, in your waking state. In what other way can you explain the absurd dreams which are dreamed by both the wisest and by the most foolish of mankind? Bad spirits, also make use of dreams to torment weak and timid souls.

"You will see, ere long, the development of another kind of dream, a kind which is as ancient as the one you know, but one of which you are ignorant. The dream we allude to is that of Jeanne Darc, of Jacob, of the Jewish prophets, and of certain Hindu ascetics: a dream which is the remembrance of the soul's experiences while entirely freed from the body, the remembrance of the second life, of which I spoke just now.

"You should carefully endeavor to distinguish these two kinds of dreams among those which you are able to recall: unless you do this, you will be in danger of falling into contradictions and errors that would be prejudicial to your belief."

Dreams are a product of the emancipation of the soul, rendered more active by the suspension of the 'active' life of relation, and enjoying a sort of indefinite clairvoyance which extends to places at a great distance from us, or that we have never seen, or even to other worlds. To this state of emancipation is also due the remembrance which retraces to our memory the events that have occurred in our present existence or in preceding existences; the strangeness of the images of what has taken place in worlds unknown to us, mixed up with the things of the present world, producing the confused and whimsical medleys that seem to be equally devoid of connection and of meaning.

The incoherence of dreams is still further explained by the 'gap' resulting from the Incompleteness of our remembrance of what has appeared to us in our nightly visions: an incompleteness similar to that of a narrative from which whole sentences, or parts of sentences, have been omitted by chance, and whose remaining fragments, having been thrown together again at random, have lost all intelligible meaning.

403. Why do we not always remember our dreams?

"What you call sleep is only the repose of the

body, for the spirit is always in motion. During sleep he recovers a portion of his liberty, and enters into communication with those who are dear to him, either in this world, or in other worlds; but as the matter of the body is heavy and gross, it is difficult for him to retain, on waking, the impressions he has received during sleep, because those impressions were not received by him through the bodily organs."

Kardec, Allan. *The Spirits' Book.* **Trans. [into English] by Anna Blackwell. São Paulo: LAKE-Livraria Allan Kardec Editora, undated. Pp. 206-207.**

Chapter 40

The Desk at the Prayer Spiritist Group

Chico serves people at the Prayer Spiritist Group, which he founded. His psychographs, which bring hope and comfort to thousands of people, would continue well into the early hours of dawn. We had the great joy, on several occasions, of being invited by Chico to sit at his desk and speak about the Gospel with other participants while he did his psychographing.

To break paradigms and to reinforce the understanding that we should not be prisoners to form, but rather should pay attention to the essence, he used an old-fashioned kitchen-style plastic tablecloth with enormous flowers that were already yellowed by time.

On one of these occasions, I had the pleasure of

meeting Carlos Baccelli and his wife Márcia, as well as Dr. Inácio Ferreira, who has been on the spiritual plane since 1988. Dr. Inácio Ferreira's books have been written, and are still being written, through the psychography of the medium Carlos Baccelli.

Sometimes we were able to verify that while Chico psychgraphed, threads of ectoplasm would come out of his nostrils. Later on, we were informed that his spiritual friends use that material given up by the medium, the ectoplasm, to work real cures on many of the people in attendance. What a great donation! How much did Chico have! Besides the long hours that he worked on psychographing, he donated ectoplasm to help the needy.

On a certain night, Chico psychographed for around eleven hours, from 8:00 pm. on Saturday to around 7:00 am on Sunday. Chico himself commented to D. Yolanda, our leader, about an experience he had that morning when he opened his eyes after so many hours of psychographing. Remember that the medium psychographed with his eyes closed.

Chico said, "You know, Yolanda, when I opened my eyes that Sunday morning, I began to see everything very clearly. It looked like everything was shining (it was the sunlight coming through his windows) so that I thought: 'My God, I think I have disincarnated! Everything is so clear and bright!'"

Chico was really a fantastic person. A friend of ours said very appropriately: "This is Chico's century. Look, he started it and he is going to end it." In fact, that's the twentieth century. Chico was born in 1910 and disincarnated in 2002, going through the twentieth century and entering the twenty-first.

Chico Xavier at the Prayer Spiritist Group

Chapter 41

The Cockroach

A very interesting episode demonstrates Chico's power of concentration and discipline, during the mediunic process. It also shows the great respect that the medium had toward the communicating spirits, in that he took great effort not to interrupt the psychography process.

It was summer in Uberaba and that Saturday night was especially hot. The Prayer Spiritist Group, as usual, was full. Chico was wearing a simple, light-colored suit, without a tie due to the great heat. During his first psychographs, an unfortunate cockroach, one of those big ones, robust and well-nourished with vitamins, crawled up one of his pant legs, beginning an anguishing climb. It went up and up until it reached the waist.

And Chico? Psychographing...

The cockroach found a loose spot at the waist between the medium's pants and shirt, inside. Chico normally wore comfortable clothes that were a little wide. And, the insect's climb continued above his waist, not in a straight line, of course. It wandered around, disoriented, poor thing, probably looking for a way out of that great adventure.

And Chico? Psychographing...

I don't know about you, my reader, but if it were me, a simple scribe and teller of "cases," I would probably have jumped out of the chair, scaring everyone in the room.

The thing went round and round so much that it ended up finding an exit in the opening of the shirt collar. That was when Mr. Weaker Batista, an old companion of our Chico, saw the insect and quickly removed it.

And Chico? Psychographing...

BIBLIOGRAPHICAL REFERENCES FOR RESEARCH
Concentration

... consists of setting our attention on a goal located inside us. Mental discipline is the key to good concentration.

Currículo para as Escolas de Evangelização. 2nd

ed. Rio de Janeiro: FEB, 1998 [*Curriculum for Schools of Evangelization*]

Discipline

Discipline is the soul of efficiency.

Bozzano, Ernesto. *Xenoglossia: Mediunidade Poliglota.* Trans. from Italian by Guillon Ribeiro. 5th ed. Rio de Janeiro: FEB, 2005. [*Xenoglossia: Polyglot Mediumship*]

Do you not believe that discipline is the best way to educate ourselves and dignify our feelings?

Xavier, Francisco Cândido. *E a Vida Continua.* By the Spirit André Luiz. 30th ed. Rio de Janeiro: FEB, 2004. [*And Life Goes On*]

Chapter 42

The Verses of Jair Presente

It was a Saturday in the month of December. The work of food distribution during Christmas week had ended, and we had served some 20,000 people, as reported by the Military Police of Uberaba.

We were at work in the Prayer Spiritist Group and Chico was psychographing...

I felt particularly exhausted, having gone almost 24 hours without rest. I began to question my work, which was and continues to be very simple in the Spiritist field. I say this with a complete knowledge of the cause and without false humility.

Due to my tiredness and lack of vigilance, I left the way open to thoughts of giving up, which grew in my mind. Already beaten down by the negative energies emitted, I began to question several aspects of the social work we had done.

Chico ended the last psychograph of the night. It was signed by the Spiritist poet Jair Presente. He spoke of charity and the activities of the groups working on the Christmas distribution that had ended a few hours earlier. He thanked everyone in the name of spirituality and then presented his verses.

On my part, I continued having the same negative thoughts, the tiredness...

But life always has surprises for us. Vigilant, attentive brothers call our attention so we may return to the correct path. They attempt to help us abandon discouraging and long-suffering attitudes that do no good. In short, they shook us up in order to wake us up.

The slap with kid-leather gloves did not take long, because soon one of Jair's verses reminded me of my responsibility as a worker for Christ. It doesn't matter how big the task is, but rather, the love with which we undertake it. We must assume our responsibilities. How long are we going to continue fooling ourselves as Spiritists committed to working for Jesus? Of course Jair Presente would not be indelicate, but with great polish and in a very simple way, he gave his message for someone who understands well, such that a single word would suffice:

"Firm and vigilant young man in charity. Long live! Here comes our brother, Umberto Fabbri."

That was quite enough for me to try to control my thoughts.

Working in service of one's neighbor, we find great joy and satisfaction. It does not matter when or where, but rather, just having the opportunity to work. We are thankful for and appreciate the blessed opportunity given by God in this reincarnation.

When I spoke with a friend of mine, I got the final lesson, because he looked at me and said: "Have you learned now?"

BIBLIOGRAPHICAL REFERENCES FOR RESEARCH

Lack of Vigilance

Thus comes the inestimable importance of the evangelical recommendation: Pray and be vigilant! It was a lack of vigilance that betrayed Peter, in spite of his close identity with Jesus. That was what led him to deny the Master three times. It is through lack of vigilance that we miss the greatest opportunities to exemplify what we have learned, and spread the Doctrine and the Gospel.

Mendes, Idalício. *Rumos Doutrinários*. 3rd ed. Rio de Janeiro: FEB, 2005. [*Doctrinal Pathways*]

Service

Service is working for good. It is making charity dynamic and achieving comprehension. It is the externalization of charity, in all its imaginable forms, toward our neighbor. The greatest example was left to us by Jesus, in his works, while he taught that he had come to serve and not to be served.

To serve righteously, we need to understand, accept, and love. At every hour, we come across opportunities to serve. We don't take advantage of them because we have selfishness within us, the moral wound that must be removed.

De Souza, Juvanir Borges. *Tempo de Transição.* **2nd ed. Rio de Janeiro: FEB, 1990.** [*Time of Transition*]

Service will always be the great renovator of our conscious life, enabling us to perform reconstructive services under the inspiration of our Divine Master and Lord.

Xavier, Francisco Cândido. *Intruções Psicofônicas.* **By diverse Spirits. 8th ed. Rio de Janeiro: FEB, 2005.** [*Psycophonic Instructions*]

Spiritist Social Service

... all Spiritist centers should perform Spiritist social service, assuring its beneficent, preventive, and promotional characteristics, bringing together material and spiritual aid, carrying out this service while attending to the needs of evangelization.

Conselho Federativo Nacional. *Orientação ao Centro Espírita.* **6th ed. Rio de Janeiro: FEB, 2004.** [*Directions for a Spiritist Center*]

To Serve

Serving, in the Christian sense, is to forget about oneself and dedicate one's efforts to helping one's neighbor, without seeking any compensation, not even recognition from those who have benefitted.

Calligaris, Rodolfo. *Parábolas Evangélicas: À Luz do Espiritismo.* **8th ed. Rio de Janeiro: FEB, 2004.** [*Gospel Parables: In the Light of Spiritism*]

Chapter 43

Visit to the Cemetery

Sometimes, while doing good works, we come upon unusual events, and we are surprised at some of the work being done to serve our fellow human beings.

We were with Chico at his home around two o'clock in the morning, when he told us that when he was young, and his legs didn't have circulation problems making it difficult to take long walks, he would often visit the city cemetery on Sunday afternoons.

Between feeling anxious, and curious to hear more about these visits, I asked a simple question: "Did you go to the cemetery to pray, Chico?"

"Yes, I also said prayers for our discarnate brethren."

"Also?"

"Yes. For many people who still did not understand

the process of disincarnation, I would ask the mentors to help them to understand, within their ability, their current condition. We met some discarnate souls who did not understand that they had left their physical bodies, and they approached us, wanting to converse."

I confess that I was amazed at this story. Chico left his house to go to the cemetery and teach the recently deceased. My God! What an exceptional person he was. He had so much love in his heart that, on a day when he could be resting, he used his time to do a work of charity, which was very unique.

But curiosity knocked at the door once again and I asked:

"Chico, what was the status of these brothers?"

"You know, Umberto, many times these brothers of ours showed themselves to be in a very difficult situation, actually carrying marks of decomposition, because they were still so mentally tied to their dead bodies. Real prisoners of themselves, as André Luiz has shown us in Obreiros da Vida Eterna, [Workers for Eternal Life] Chapter 15, "Learning Always."

"Naturally, no one is forgotten by Divine Mercy, and these brothers are supported by spiritual friends, within the capabilities and merit of each one. Our Father loves all, equally, and does not abandon us at any time in our lives."

BIBLIOGRAPHICAL REFERENCES FOR RESEARCH

Perturbation in Disincarnation

In the transition from bodily life to spiritual life, another phenomenon occurs of capital importance: Perturbation in disincarnation. At that moment the soul feels a weakness that momentarily paralyzes his faculties, neutralizing the sensations, at least in part... This perturbation may be considered the normal state at the instant of death, and it may last for an indeterminate length of time, varying from a few hours to a few years. As it becomes free, the soul finds itself in a situation comparable to that of a man who awakens from a profound sleep, with confused, vague, uncertain ideas; his vision changes is as if through a fog, but slowly becomes clear, as the memory and knowledge of himself returns. This awakening can be quite diverse: calm for some, bringing about delicious sensations; gloomy, terrifying and anxious for others, like a horrid nightmare.

O Céu e o Inferno ou A Justiça Divina Segundo o Espiritismo. **Trans. by Alceu Nunes. São Paulo: Edições FEESP, 2011.** [*Heaven and Hell or Divine Justice According to Spiritism*]

Chapter 44

Antusa and Her Blessings

Our experiences were not reserved to our dear Chico, but also involved other people who surrounded him. It would be an injustice to try to list them all because we would certainly miss some, and we would end up forgetting about some very important persons in Uberaba and other cities. However, one person stands out.

We had the opportunity to meet Antusa Ferreira. Our first visit occurred on a Saturday morning, when we were invited to meet her, and to receive a blessing from her enlightened hands.

Antusa has been on the spiritual plane for many years now. This worker for Jesus was a very special person, so much so that Chico himself insisted on leaving his home and going to her residence to receive a blessing from her.

She was a middle-aged woman, poor, living in a wooden house [considered inferior to brick in Brazil]; at the back of her lot there was a tiny shack, also of made of wood, surrounded by a garden, which was full of flowers year-round, exhaling a perfume that caught the attention of everyone who visited. It was in this shack that Antusa gave her blessings and said her prayers for the work with Jesus.

This valiant worker for Jesus had physical limitations. She was deaf and mute, but she spoke with gestures and with her soft, loving eyes. She had impressive energy, which surrounded everyone in vibrations of well-being and indescribable joy. It is worth noting, that her personal magnetism was contagious and it brought everyone into a climate of peace, not to mention the blessings themselves, which were true founts of energy and health.

One of the most interesting things about her mediumship was her ability to leave her body. Many people took her photographs of relatives or friends, and Antusa would look at the photos and give precise diagnoses of the people in the pictures, as well as the necessary treatment. This would happen in fractions of a second, between looking and gesticulating on how to proceed with the treatment, whether spiritual, medical, or... That simple, modest woman referred to Chico as her dear friend from other incarnations.

Whoever got to know Chico intimately can confirm that, as we have said previously, he was not a simple medium, but rather a missionary spirit of great bearing, who got along with people of all levels of society, from presidents to the simplest of souls, in a respectful, brotherly way, as do all the greatest of souls.

BIBLIOGRAPHICAL REFERENCES FOR RESEARCH

Blessing by the laying on of hands

In the form of the blessing, magnetism is widely used today, mainly at Spiritist centers.

In the present-day liturgy of the Catholic Church, 'the blessing' can also be identified in the laying on of hands of the godmothers and godfathers in certain marriage and baptismal ceremonies. We will also find it in exorcisms and in blessings in general.

According to the Spiritist vision, it is always a fluidic-magnetic process, which has the primary objective of helping to restore the organic balance of the patient. By 'organic' we mean the complete structure of the individual, when discarnate, the spirit and perispirit;

when incarnate, the physical body, the astral body, perispirit and spirit.

The blessing can be given by an incarnate spirit, by a discarnate spirit, or even by the joint action of an incarnate and a discarnate...

As we shall see below, at certain times we will have to proceed to the removal, and at other times, to the concentration, of fluids in the patient. These two types of actions characterize the two very different stages that normally need to be executed. One is the stage of removal of fluids, generally called the "dispersion phase," and the other is the supply of fluids, the "donation phase."

We should begin with the dispersion phase-cleaning the fluidic field of the patient-attempting to remove all harmful fluids that surround him, and only later begin the donation of fluids. If this sequence is inverted, we are going to waste fluids by dispersing the fluids that we are donating. This basic rule can never be ignored: first the dispersion and then the donation.

As we execute the dispersion as the initial phase of the blessing, we will be preventing the fluids donated in the next phase from being repelled by the fluidic envelope of the patient, as a result of the repulsion between fluids of a naturally opposing nature: the

Fundamental Law of Fluids. This phase, therefore, demands maximum attention.

After donation, one must not proceed to any maneuvers that would lead to the dispersion of the donated fluids.

It is important to observe that, in the donation phase, the beneficial fluids are only made available to the patient. We say 'available' because in fact, speaking precisely, that is what happens, since absorption of these fluids may not be guaranteed. The absorption of fluids depends on many factors - some totally beyond the control of the person who is giving the blessing - the most significant of these is, and always will be, the receptivity of the patient. If he puts himself in a sufficient state of receptivity, he will easily absorb the fluids that the blessing giver has made available. Otherwise, absorption will not take place, or will be greatly reduced.

Gurgel, Luiz Carlos de M. *O Passe Espírita*. 5th ed. Rio de Janeiro: FEB, 2006. [*The Spiritist Blessing*]

... blessings, [are] like transfusions of psychic forces, in which precious spiritual energies flow from the messengers of Christ to the donors and beneficiaries, [and] represent the continuity of effort by the Master to attenuate the suffering of the world.

Xavier, Francisco Cândido. *Caminho, Verdade e Vida.* **By the Spirit Emmanuel. 26th ed. Rio de Janeiro: FEB, 2006.** [*The Way, Truth, and Life*]

The blessing is a transfusion of energies, altering the cellular field... In magnetic assistance, the spiritual resources get involved between emission and reception, helping the needy person to help himself. The reanimated mind raises up again the microscopic lives that serve it, in the temple of the body... The blessing, as we recognize, is an important contribution for one who knows how to receive it, with respect to having confidence in it and recognizing its value.

Xavier, Francisco Cândido. *Nos Domínios da Mediunidade.* **By the Spirit André Luiz. 32nd ed. Rio de Janeiro: FEB, 2005.** [*In the Domains of Mediumship*]

When the hands, the mind, and the heart are united, we favor donations of energy that harmonize the perispirit, and disconnect from the negative, and balance the systems and organ functions. We execute a task of great importance, benefiting the receivers and ourselves. In living with spiritual mentors, in such a praiseworthy act, we experience feelings of indescribable triumph.

Anselmo, Maria de Cássia et al. *Estudo e Prática de Assistência Espiritual.* São Paulo: Edições FEESP, 2012. [*Study and Practice of Spiritual Assistance*]

Chapter 45

Mrs. Aparecida and the Pênfigo Hospital

Every time those of us from the Augusto Cezar Home Workshop visited Chico, we reserved Saturday afternoon to visit the Pênfigo Hospital in Uberaba.

Mrs. Aparecida had impressive mediumship, which gave a different tone to the place and, of course, to our visits.

Right away, on our first visit, we had the opportunity to meet one of the patients in the hospital, whose name was José, or "Zé" as he was known. He had serious mental problems, and among all of his difficulties, the most marked, and that which we most noticed, was that he always walked backwards. He leaned against walls, which he used as a guide to be able to walk without falling. Undoubtedly, he was a person of great trials.

On one of our visits to the hospital, one of our companions asked about Zé's situation. "What could that spirit have done to experience a trial of that nature?"

Mrs. Aparecida, with the simplicity that was so characteristic of her, responded quickly: "Zé is the reincarnation of Mussolini!"

Our friend was amazed.

"You refer to Mussolini? The Il Duce?"

She answered: "The very one, my son, Mussolini himself." And she continued, "Divine Mercy acts in favor of all of us. He is not here in that condition as punishment. He is hidden! There still exist a number of discarnate spirits that are looking for him in Europe. How could they imagine that they would find him here in his condition? In the Pênfigo Hospital, in Uberaba, in a reincarnation as a black man with serious deficiencies?"

"Why would God permit the continuation of a wave of hate and vengeance?"

"Hiding him here reduces the wrath of those who thirst for vengeance. All are sick like him. With time they will feel the need to care for their own lives, working in favor of evolution, and our friend has just begun to follow the same path here."

Really, everything that Mrs. Aparecida told us made sense. We remember that André Luiz had related the case of a nobleman hidden in a totally compromised body, in the interior of Brazil.

Our colleague in the group continued to insist: "Mrs. Aparecida, have you confirmed this vision of yours with anyone, about the reincarnation of our brother?"

"With Chico, my son, with Chico!"

BIBLIOGRAPHICAL REFERENCES FOR RESEARCH

Stationary Debt

... A few minutes later, we found ourselves in a poor, sad, rural passageway. In a hut, totally exposed to the night winds, an unfortunate woman lay rolled up in rags, on a straw mat on the ground, and a few feet away was a miserable paralytic dwarf with a plain, ashen face. We recognized him immediately as seriously mentally challenged, under the watch of the unfortunate sick woman, who looked at him with affliction and disappointment.

Seeing them, our guide informed us in a solicitous manner:

"Here we have our sister Pollyanna and Sabino, the

unfortunate son that the Heavenly Power bestowed upon her. Spiritually, they are both in the custody of the Mansion, on a rocky road of readjustment."

... Then, he invited us to observe Sabino's organic field.

Outside, there he was, a painful mask of abnormality and aberration. Withered up, measuring no more than thirty-five inches in height, with an enlarged head, the deformed body emitted stinking odors, he stirred feelings of both compassion and repugnance. His countenance suggested that of a primate, however, he showed in his unconscious smile and his semi-lucid eyes the expression of a sad clown.

The Assistant recommended that we listen to his intimate field, and because of this, after a few minutes of reflection, I was able to assimilate his mental banner, observing in him singular reminiscences... Showing us that he was living far away from reality. Sabino's memories were all flooded with strange pictures.

Brought to life by our spiritual vision, his thoughts took form, compelling us to look at what he really felt. We saw him in palatial clothes, well-positioned, manipulating people to perform concealed crimes that always ended in their flagellation. Widows and orphans, humble workers and miserable slaves, filed across the screens of his complicated memories. Aristocratic palaces and splendid tables were among the Faustian details of the memories that populated his spirit... And, at his side, always the same woman, whose proud bearing revealed Pollyanna, that same Pollyanna who lay inert on the straw mat... Surprised, we identified the two of them surrounded by luxury and gold, stained, however, by blood, to which they were fully indifferent.

We recognized that they carried serious commitments to each other, in the land of cruelty. Sabino, the proud noble, did not take notice of Sabino, the paralytic dwarf. In complete introspection, he relived the past, with adornments of self-adoration, showing himself to be a man with the delusion of false superiority over others.

Noticing our perplexity, Silas observed:

"Certainly, we shall not hear him articulate words, deaf and mute as he is, but we can consult his thoughts, as he will react in thought, responding to our questions through idealized conversation. For that purpose, however, it is essential that we use the proper form of address to the personality that he believes he is... Let us imagine him as being the Baron of S-, the title that he had in his last existence, and with which he ruinously hallucinated in the darkness of delinquency and vanity.

Observing the reddish stains on the living pictures of the memories in which he had cloistered himself, we asked with the natural gravity that experience demanded:

"Baron, why is there so much blood on your path? Have many people cried about their march?"

I noticed that he did not pick up the question with his regular eardrums, but he understood it in the form of an idea, formulated by him for himself, returning to us the following thought by mental threads, without identifying myself as his invisible interlocutor. "Blood and tears, yes! ... I needed a large dose of similar material in my undertakings. What triumphant leader of the world will not have blood and tears at the base of the pyramids of fortune or political domination that support all of them? Life is a system of struggle, in which humanity is divided into two opposing camps those that conquer and those that are conquered... I am a nobleman... I do not have the inclination to lose... What does the affliction of the weak matter, if death means for them rest and mercy?"

I disconnected myself from the mental focus in which thoughts were being expressed, and after a few moments, in which Hilário dedicated himself to the same examination that had drawn my attention, the Assistant explained:

As it is easy to conclude, from the viewpoint of common earthly science, Sabino is a paralytic idiot, deaf and mute from birth... For us, however, he is a prisoner who is still dangerous, caged in physical bones, the composition of which he has no notion, such is the selfishness that still roils his soul, in a process of uncontrollable hypertrophy.... His thirst for ignoble possession and virulent pride have perverted his interior life, putting him in a frightening labyrinth of sinister deception, which results in complete mental alienation in time; instead of the clock moving forward in counting the days, he will remain stuck in the reminiscences in which he supposes himself to be the dominator on Earth, living the nightmare that he himself created.

In view of the problems that the study brought up, Hilário asked, surprised:

"But... what is the advantage of such suffering?"

Silas showed a slight expression of sadness and considered:

We have under our attention a lamentable frozen debt. Our poor companion, deplorably fallen, performed many crimes on Earth and on the Spiritual Plane, and, for more than a thousand years, he has been yielding, vain and careless, to the claws of criminality... From existence to existence, he knew only how to consume the resources of the physical field, making turmoil within the social pathways that the Lord had given him to live in. Diverse crimes, such as murders, rebellion, extortion, calumnies, bankruptcies, suicides, abortions, and obsessions were caused by him for many centuries, while he saw nothing before his eyes but his unending selfishness... Between the crib and the tomb, it is incessant folly, from the tomb to the crib, it is cold and inconsequential evil, in spite of the intercessions of self-sacrificing friends, who have supported him in new attempts at regeneration and ascendency.

Almost always inspired by the ideas of Pollyanna, who has been his companion through multiple journeys, he became crystalized as an ill-fated entrepreneur of crime, the disequilibrium becoming so large in their last existence, which ended in their indirect suicide through deliberate submersion into vice, that there was no other solution for him than absolute isolation in the flesh, to the state of his present pilgrimage. In which we now identify him, like this, a beast caged in a degrading cell, under the watch of the woman who helped him become this, now lifted to the position of a maternal nursemaid of his long misfortune. Pollyanna, the useless companion far-removed from goodness, who habitually chose the position of a model of criminal inclination, awoke, beyond the grave, to the realities of life, before him... She awoke and suffered a lot, accepting the task of helping him in the recovery in which, certainly, he will spend a great deal more time.

In the perispiritual field of the introverted dwarf, we observe through his dark green aura, that all the energies of his vibratory fulcra flow back to their origin, giving us the impression that Sabino was involved completely in himself, like a worm isolated in the cocoon which he himself made.

Silas quickly answered the questions that it was not possible for us to ask:

"Our friend, until he matures in spirit for the necessary renewal, will keep his mind working in a closed circuit, that is, thinking constantly about himself, incapable of exchanging vibrations with others, except for Pollyanna, whom he made into a mute and eager satellite, like a parasite on a sappy leaf. Sabino is a problem of stationary debt, because he lies in spiritual hibernation, necessarily enveloped in his own interior, for the benefit of the community of discarnate and incarnate spirits. So long as he continues to carry the material and moral burdens that his conscious presence, on Earth or in space, would cause unforeseeable turmoil. He is enjoying, in this way, a pause in the struggle, like a trial of forgetfulness, in order that he may, in the future, face the sum of his commitments, finding a worthy solution for them in coming centuries, in the fight of self-renunciation."

"But," asked Hilário, disturbed, "wouldn't superior Spirituality have tools available to incarcerate him, at a distance from the flesh?"

"Yes," confirmed Silas, "that is not impossible. However, if we have powerful dungeons for the atonement of crimes that darken the human mind, many of them expressed through vales of misery and horror, it is necessary to consider that the criminals attract each other, mutually infecting each other with the moral wounds that they carry, generating the hell in which they are temporarily living. On the other hand, we have many institutions which function like greenhouses, in which incarnate creatures sleep peacefully in long naps, submerged in the nightmares that they deserve, up to a certain point, after they have made the passage from the sepulcher... In Sabino, however, we find an exceptional case of systematic rebellion and delinquency, in whose shadows, one day, he felt his forces falter. Remorse wounded his heart as a mortal bullet assaults a loose tiger. Prayer came into his conscience and, before his new attitude could provoke reactions and useless punishments among those that followed his perverse lead, some got together in the Mansion, where they were naturally magnetized, falling into long-term hypnosis, and received later by the affection of Pollyanna, they then segregated him in a regeneration camp for sacrifice. As we see, so great are the connections of our companion to the infernal planes that, by the mercy of Jesus, he was provisionally hidden in this monstrous body which is not only incommunicable, but also unrecognizable, as a service to him. It is crucial that time with Divine Goodness will support his afflictive and complex problems."

And, looking at us serenely, he added:

"Did you understand?"

Yes, we had understood. Experience, to our eyes, was hard but logical, terrible but just.

And because there was nothing more we could do for our sad friend, beyond the heart, Silas rubbed his dirty head and offered him, with emotion, the blessing of a prayer.

Xavier, Francisco Cândido. *Ação e Reação.* By the Spirit André Luiz. 26th ed. Rio de Janeiro: FEB, 2006. Chapter 13 "Débito Estacionário." [*Action and Reaction*, 'Stationary Debt']

Chapter 46

A Mother's Heart

We were talking with Chico about the number of women who sought him out in Uberaba, at the Prayer Spiritist Group, looking for messages from their sons or daughters, who had disincarnated, when the medium told us: "I may understand the suffering of a mother's heart in such a difficult trial, as is the departure of a child, especially when they are very young. I feel in my heart the pain that the mothers experience. I remember that I lived a similar experience in one of my incarnations."

We looked at each other and one of the members of our group asked: "Chico, could you say something about that experience?"

"Yes, it was in Spain. In that existence, I reincarnated as a woman and I married a very rich and influential man. We lived a comfortable life when we were blessed with the arrival of a little child, who came along to complete our happiness. With the passing of the years, he was being primed to manage our fortune. When was about 19 years old, to our great sadness, he was kidnapped. Our despair was terrible until we received the first contact from his abductors, asking for a ransom. It was a large amount, but we were rich, so we had no difficulty in coming up with the amount demanded and we paid it.

"After making the payment, we went to get our beloved son, at the place indicated by the kidnappers. Those were moments of extreme anguish that turned into terrible pain. When we went to the place, we found our son lifeless. He had been brutally murdered by the kidnappers, in spite of our compliance with all of their demands.

"And it is for that reason that I can understand the pain of a mother's heart in search of her beloved son."

That moment was one of silence and emotion, without our being able to say or ask anything.

BIBLIOGRAPHICAL REFERENCES FOR RESEARCH
Heart

... the heart is more than a pump that pushes blood through the organism.

Being the most resistant physiological organ known to the thinking being, since it begins to beat in the twenty-fifth day of life of the fetus, it continues in action palpitating one hundred thousand times every day, which results in forty million times per year, and when it ceases, life becomes disorganized, resulting in the death of the organic equipment with its consequent degeneration.

Little by little, scientists are realizing that it is the carrier of a vital energy that keeps it and impels it without interruption. That energy would be permutable, possibly being interchanged with other individuals who would benefit or not, according to the level of its constitution, positive or negative, warm or cold, stimulating or indifferent.

According to this line of reasoning, they are concluding that that organ is the carrier of the faculty of thought, affirming the traditional 'voice of the heart' to which poets, writers, artists, lovers... and Jesus refer.

Franco, Divaldo P. *Impermanência e Imortalidade.* **By the Spirit Carlos Torres Pastorino. 4th ed. Rio de Janeiro: FEB, 2005.** [*Impermanence and Immortality*]

Mother's Heart

The mother's heart is a cup of love in which life is manifest in the world.

Xavier, Francisco Cândido. *Libertação.* **By the Spirit André Luiz. 29th ed. Rio de Janeiro: FEB, 2005. [*Liberation*]**

Also by the author, in Portuguese

Cisco Cândido Xavier

Nascer de Novo

Eu, imigrante

Mediunidade, Ferramenta Divina

Recomeçar a Viver

www.ingramcontent.com/pod-product-compliance
Lightning Source LLC
Chambersburg PA
CBHW061630040426
42446CB00010B/1342